A Guide to Early Years Practice

Many changes have taken place in early years education since the publication of the second edition of this book. This fully revised new edition places particular emphasis on *Birth to Three Matters*, the new Childcare Bill and the development of children's centres, and has additional focus on the Foundation Stage Profile and its relationship to the proposed Early Years Foundation Stage.

This accessible text also offers:

- practical advice on how to successfully involve parents as equal partners in the education of their children;
- detailed discussion of the Foundation Stage, the proposed Early Years Foundation Stage and early learning goals;
- guidance to ensure that the activities and support offered to young children will promote learning across a broad and balanced early years curriculum;
- a particular focus on special needs, multiculturalism and multilingualism, play and culture, and the importance of interactions with adults and with peers.

A Guide to Early Years Practice is essential reading for students on early years courses, and anyone concerned with the care and education of young children. Practitioners can also use this text as the starting point for developing their own methods within the frameworks of statutory documents relating to early years education.

Sandra Smidt was previously Principal Lecturer in Early Years Education, University of East London, and has also authored *Observing, Assessing and Planning for Children in the Early Years* and *The Developing Child in the 21st Century: A Global Perspective on Child Development*, both published by Routledge.

A Guide to Early Years Practice

Third Edition

Sandra Smidt

Routledge
Taylor & Francis Group

LONDON AND NEW YORK

First edition published 1998
Second edition published 2002
This edition published 2007
by Routledge
2 Park Square, Milton Park, Abingdon, Oxon OX14 4RN

Simultaneously published in the USA and Canada
by Routledge
270 Madison Ave, New York, NY 10016

Routledge is an imprint of the Taylor & Francis Group, an informa business

Typeset in Garamond and Gill by BC Typesetting Ltd, Bristol
Printed and bound in Great Britain by
MPG Books Ltd, Bodmin

British Library Cataloguing in Publication Data
A catalogue record for this book is available from the British Library

Library of Congress Cataloging in Publication Data
Smidt, Sandra, 1943–
    A guide to early years practice/Sandra Smidt.–3rd ed.
      p. cm.
    Includes bibliographical references.
    ISBN-13: 978–0–415–41604–7 (pbk.)
    ISBN-10: 0–415–41604–3 (pbk.)
    1. Early childhood education–Great Britain. 2. Child development–
Great Britain. I. Title.

  LB1139 3.3.G7S65 2007
  372.210941–dc22   200602108

ISBN10: 0–415–41604–3
ISBN13: 978–0–415–41604–7

For Hannah, Ben, Chloe, Jake and Zac

Contents

Chapter 1

Understanding how young children learn best

Michael Chung is four years old. He goes to playgroup four mornings a week. At home his family speak Cantonese and English, and Michael is fluent in both languages. One morning Michael arrives at playgroup. He takes off his coat and hangs it on his peg. He greets all the adults and heads straight for the home corner. He selects a doll, carefully undresses the doll and then places the doll in a plastic bucket of water in order to bath her. He holds the doll in one arm whilst he pretends to squeeze shampoo from an empty bottle on the doll's head. He rubs the head gently, using one hand to shield the doll's eyes and all the time he talks to the doll in a crooning voice, saying things like 'Don't cry. It will be all right. It will be nice and clean.' When he is satisfied that the doll is clean, he lifts her out of the water, wraps her in a towel and starts to dress her. First he puts on a disposable nappy, then a vest, then a 'babygro'. That done, he picks up an empty feeding bottle and begins to feed the baby, this time singing to her. Finally, he puts the doll on his shoulder, pats her back and puts her down in a box which serves as a cot. Then he leaves the home corner, and goes over to a table where writing materials have been set out. He selects a blank booklet and begins to make marks on the pages, working from the front of the booklet to the back. Finally he takes a pencil and carefully writes his name on the front of the booklet and places it in the pocket of his coat to take home.

An everyday event in any playgroup, nursery or group. Nothing that Michael did was remarkable or surprising, and most people observing Michael would have said that he was playing in the way most young children play. But this little vignette tells us quite a lot about Michael and gives us an insight into what he already knows, what he can do, what he is interested in and how he chooses to spend his time. Information like this is essential to anyone working with young children.

In this opening chapter we will look at what is currently known about how young children learn – and, most crucially, we will examine theories about how young children learn best. We do know that young children can be taught to do many things in many different ways. Our concern is to examine the best ways to promote learning in young children.

What we mean by learning

'Learning' is a word we all use frequently and often without really considering what it means. It is a word we use to describe an enormous range of experiences and events.

Think about these statements:

'I learned, early on, that I wanted to be famous.'
'Children learn through play.'
'When I first learned to read I couldn't get enough books.'
'Jamie learned to talk at nine months.'
'I learned to drive.'
'At school I had to learn poetry off by heart.'
'I never learned another language.'
'I used to hate olives, but then I learned to love them.'

If you analyse each of these you will find that we sometimes use the word 'learning' to talk about how we acquire skills – learning to drive, to walk or to use a knife and fork, for example. We use the word to talk about how we acquire attitudes – learning to enjoy the books or appreciate the taste of olives. We use the word to describe how we appreciate how to relate to other people. In short, the word 'learning' is a broad term that defines what happens to us in a range of circumstances and over an indefinite period of time. You will know that children learn at home, in the playground, at school, in the streets. Learning happens all the time.

What some people believe is actually happening when we learn is that connections between cells in the brain are laid down and strengthened. So, 'learning' also has a very precise meaning. At birth, the human infant has all the brain cells needed for human development. In order for the human being to function, however, connections or pathways need to be formed between these cells. You will have read that learning during the first five years of life is more rapid than at any other time. This is why the early years of life are said to be so crucial in terms of learning.

Some research has shown that these neural pathways are formed most effectively through experience. Each time a child encounters something new and interesting, the child explores the new object or situation, and as he or she does, connections between brain cells are laid down. However, there are dangers in just accepting this statement without more careful consideration.

Most of the research done has been done on privileged children from privileged backgrounds. Certainly children learn through their experiences, but not only children from privileged backgrounds learn. A learning experience can be going for a walk by the river, making chapattis with your mum, helping in the house or sitting quietly and looking at the sky. We need to be sure that we understand that children will learn without expensive toys or resources.

Think about all the things you have learned in the past four years. Now think about all the things that you think Michael has learned in the past four years. What do you find?

Your list might have included things like:

- learned to make meringues
- learned to use an electric drill
- learned to tango.

In the list of what Michael has learned you might have included things like:

- learned to sit
- learned to stand
- learned to walk
- learned to use both hands in conjunction
- learned to understand and speak two languages
- learned how to bath a baby
- learned how to use a pencil
- learned how to behave at playgroup.

You will realise from this how accelerated learning is in the first few years of life. As we get older we do continue learning, but the rate at which we learn decreases dramatically. And do remember that our learning does not depend on money or toys or advantage.

So, we have established that learning appears to mean something very precise in terms of what happens physiologically. Many researchers and theorists have studied the development of children, and their work is useful to those of us working with young children as it gives us a framework in which to plan our work. It also helps us to justify what we do to parents and to other workers. We will start by looking at some of the things the most influential theorists have to say, and later in this book I will refer to them to support what I am saying.

The work of Jean Piaget

We will start by looking at the work of Jean Piaget, a Swiss theorist who studied his own children and children in groups. We will start with him because he is the theorist who is best known in the United Kingdom, not because he is the most important. His work is, however, important for a number of reasons. In the first place, he was the first person to show that the human infant is not passive, but actively tries to get meaning from all the experiences he or she encounters. Prior to this, people had believed that the infant had to be 'fed' experiences, but Piaget showed that the human infant is an 'active learner'. Many people, when they first encounter this idea, think it refers to the fact that the infant is physically active and learns through this. Piaget meant, however, that the human infant is mentally or cognitively active. In other words, the human infant is busy trying to understand the world, and each experience results in changes in mental function.

To explain this, Piaget used the terms 'accommodation' and 'assimilation'. Assimilation is seen as the process of taking in new information, of adding to the existing experiences and sometimes changing these. Remember that all of this happens in the brain. Accommodation is the next stage of learning and is when the child or infant uses information in the brain in order to adapt to the environment. You will realise from this that Piaget saw accommodation as the higher-order cognitive process, the one that allows us to solve problems.

The second reason for looking at the work of Piaget is that his work has had a profound effect on the school system in England. In his work he speculated that all children passed through clearly defined stages of development. The first stage, which he called the Sensori-motor stage, lasted from birth to the age of two. The second stage – which he called the stage of Pre-operational Thought – lasted from two to about seven. The stage of Operational Thought followed and was thought to continue to the age of about eleven. The final stage, that of Formal Operations, continued into adulthood. You will realise that these stages correspond closely with the English schools system: nursery/ infant from three to seven; junior from eight to eleven; secondary from eleven to adulthood.

Now it is important to note that although Piaget's work was very important and influential, much of it has been criticised, and the largest body of criticism relates to this stage theory of development. At first glance you may think that what you have read so far makes sense. To anyone involved with children it is clear that children do develop and that the behaviour and learning of a seven-year-old are very different from those of a three-year-old. Piaget, however, tended to focus on what children could not yet do rather than looking at what they could do.

Think about the example which follows and see what you think you can deduce about what the child knows and can do and about what the child cannot yet do.

Four-year-old Rehana paints a picture at the easel, takes a pencil and makes some marks in the top right-hand corner of the page. The first mark is clearly an attempt at the 'R' with which her name begins.

If you were considering what she knows, you might say that she knows that she ought to write her name on her painting and that she knows the first letter of her name. If you were considering what she doesn't yet know, you might say that she doesn't yet know how to write her name properly. For those of us working with children it is much more important to know what children already know and can do. This allows us to plan what to offer them next in order to help them take the next step in learning.

In devising the stages, Piaget tended to focus on what children could not yet do. This is particularly true of children in the Pre-operational stage, which is the stage that most concerns us. According to Piaget, children under the age of about seven are not able to think logically or to conserve ideas of number, length, capacity or volume. Piaget's theories about this stage came from a number of experiments he did with children where he gave them tasks to do. Many of these are well known, as, for example, giving children two identical lumps of plasticine and then dividing one lump into a number of smaller lumps. The child was then asked 'Are they the same?' Younger children tended to answer that they were not the same, that the lump that had been divided up into several smaller lumps 'had more'. Some critics of Piaget point out that since the children had witnessed the adult dividing up one lump of plasticine, they must have assumed that this had to be a trick question. Other critics suggest that the children couldn't see the point of the activity or of the question and so tended to give the answer they thought the adult wanted to hear.

Piaget also said that young children in the Pre-operational stage are not able to take on the perspective of someone else. In other words, young children are what he called 'egocentric': they see themselves as being central to everything and cannot see the world from anyone else's point of view. He did not mean that young children are selfish, but that they cannot mentally put themselves into the position of someone else. To illustrate this, he carried out an experiment involving three papier mâché mountains. The young child was placed in front of these models and then a doll was put in a position offering a different view of the mountains. The children were asked to select the drawing which showed the view the doll could see. Very few of these young children were able to do this; they tended to select the picture showing the view they could see. For Piaget this was evidence enough.

How do you feel about this? Have you encountered young children who are able to demonstrate that they are able to appreciate what it feels like to be in someone else's shoes? How about the child who rushes over to comfort a friend who has fallen and grazed her knee?

Martin Hughes (cited in Donaldson 1978) tried a different experiment to demonstrate that young children are able to take on the view of someone else. Children were told that a teddy had been naughty and were then asked to hide the teddy from a policeman doll. Many of the young children were able to do this. The reasons for this are both interesting and directly relevant to our work with young children. Hughes believed that these young children were able to 'decentre' (that is, to take on the views of another) when what they were asked to do made sense to them. He also believed that young children demonstrate what they know best when they are able to draw on their previous experience. In his 'Naughty Teddy' experiment he felt that many of the young children had had experience of hiding things or of hiding themselves. They also might have had experience of being 'naughty' and could see why the teddy might need to be hidden from the policeman.

A final word about the work of Piaget. He did his work on his own children and the children of his peers and colleagues. All of these were white, privileged children – mainly boys – and the conclusions he drew cannot straightforwardly be used to apply to children as such.

A pause now, to draw breath and to pull out the two main themes of this section:

Summary
- From birth, human infants actively seek to understand their world.
- Young children learn best when they can see the purpose of what they are doing and when they are able to draw on their previous experience.

The work of Margaret Donaldson

Let us now turn to the work of a more recent theorist, Margaret Donaldson. She was one of Piaget's fiercest critics and the person who motivated Hughes in much of his research. In her book *Children's Minds*, published in 1978, she looked at how children are taught when they first start school and related it to what was known about how young children learn. The learning that children are required to do when they start formal schooling is what Donaldson called 'decontextualised', which means that it is not rooted in a context. Take, for example, children being asked to colour in a set of balloons on a worksheet. This is not something that is set in a context that makes sense to young children. Why are they being asked to do this? What purpose does it serve? Will it matter if the big balloon is red rather than blue? As a contrast, you might like to consider the young child painting spontaneously at an easel and selecting which colours to use.

Abstract learning – which describes much of the learning children do at school – is very difficult for young learners. They need to be able to draw on their previous experience and to use practical tools and activities to help them make sense of what they are doing. Of course, all children do need to be able to cope with abstract learning. We would not expect children to go through life always needing physical props and lifelike activities in order to learn. The crucial point Donaldson makes is that children need to be led gradually and gently into abstract learning and that this will happen best if children are allowed a range of experiences in settings which are familiar and which make 'human sense' to them. Donaldson calls settings like these 'meaningful contexts'.

To illustrate this more clearly, let us examine some familiar activities which can be described as meaningful contexts:

Think about these activities and see if you can say what makes each into something that could be called a 'meaningful context'.

Example 1
The children in the playgroup are baking cookies with an adult. They have been to the shops in order to buy the ingredients, and one child handed over the money to the shopkeeper and got the change. The adult had a shopping list and had told the children what ingredients they would need. Back in the playgroup each child has a mixing bowl and each is involved in beating together the ingredients, sifting the flour and spooning the mixture into cookie tins.

Example 2
The staff in the nursery have set up a baby clinic in a corner of the room. Two children have recently had baby sisters. The clinic is equipped with some posters and leaflets obtained from the local baby clinic up the road, weighing scales, a baby bath, some dolls, some clipboards, a stethoscope donated by a parent and a doll's cot.

In considering Example 1 you might have said that all children will have had experience of going to the shops. They know that you need to buy things and that that involves some exchange of money. They have probably been to the shops with someone carrying a shopping list. Moreover, all children are familiar with food, with cooking and with eating. So, it is an activity whose purpose is clear (delicious cookies to eat!) and one which is familiar.

In considering Example 2 you might have felt that many children will have had some experience of going to a clinic, and those with younger siblings may have accompanied parents to the baby clinic.

It is easy to see how activities like this are both familiar and meaningful to children. What many people find difficult to understand (and sometimes to explain to parents) is what children are actually learning as they play in settings like these. In order to answer this question we need to look more closely at what we mean by 'play'. Everyone working with young children knows that play is important. We often say things like 'Children learn through play' or 'Play is children's work'. But what do we mean by play and how can we be sure that play is so important in the early years?

The importance of play

Many researchers and theorists have written about play. You may be familiar with the books by Tina Bruce or Janet Moyles. What makes play is that it is something the child has chosen to do. So, if you tell a child to go and play with the Lego, for example, the child has not chosen to do this and what the child does cannot properly be described as play. When a child has chosen to do something, this indicates that the child is following some interest of his or her own. The child is then free to follow this interest and pursue it, often over a long period of time.

Think about this:

Hannah is thirteen months old. She is playing outdoors with a plastic bowl of water, a paintbrush, a scrubbing brush, a sieve and a small container. The adults with her have shown her how to paint with water on the yard floor. Because, like most children, she is obliging, she copies what the adults do for a few seconds. But her real interest lies elsewhere. She scuttles backwards and forwards between her mother and the plastic bowl, carrying both brushes in one hand. She hands the brushes to her mother, takes them back, returns to the bowl, places them in the water, takes them out, returns to her mother and so on. The activity lasts for more than forty minutes.

It is difficult to know what Hannah is pursuing as she plays. Perhaps she is exploring the distance between the bowl and her mother. Perhaps it is perfecting the newly developed skill of holding two objects in one hand. But what is clear is that this is something in which she is deeply engrossed and that she pursues for a long period of time. We often hear people say that young children have a 'limited concentration span'. This is only true when children are doing things they have been told to do rather than things they have chosen to do. So, the first important feature of play is that it allows children to explore their own interests and to get deeply engrossed in doing this.

Because children have chosen what they do when they play, they set their own goals. The second important feature of play is that it carries no risk of failure. The child has decided what to do and therefore cannot fail. No one has set the child goals that are too difficult or even too easy. The purpose of the play is in the child's hands. If something goes wrong, the child just changes the direction of the play.

A theorist who wrote a great deal about play was the Russian psychologist Vygotsky. He was particularly interested in two aspects of play. First, he believed that in play, particularly in imaginative play, children operate at their highest level of intellectual functioning, way beyond their everyday competence. He believed that, in play, a child stands 'a head taller' than him- or herself. What he meant by this was that when you observe a child engaged in imaginative play and pay close attention to what the child is doing, he or she demonstrates knowledge and abilities that you would not see when the child is in a different situation.

Think about the example that follows and see whether it explains what Vygotsky meant.

Johan is in the reception class. He finds it difficult to do the tasks expected of him: writing, doing number work, colouring in, and so on. But his teacher was surprised to notice that when he was out in the playground playing 'pirates' on the climbing frame he was able to express ideas, solve problems, communicate his thoughts and ideas, and negotiate with the other children. In his imaginative play he stood 'a head taller' than he appeared in the classroom.

The second aspect of play that interested Vygotsky was how, through play, children begin to understand what is called 'the symbolic function'. A symbol is something that stands for or represents something else. Our spoken language is symbolic. The word 'dog' stands for or represents the living creature. Our written language is symbolic. The letters 'd-o-g' stand for that same living creature. Our number system is symbolic. The symbol '2' means more than one and less than three. In order to live in the real world, all children need to come to understand how one thing can stand for another.

In imaginative play, children, from very early on, begin to use one thing to represent another. The young child who places a block to her ear and pretends it is a telephone is doing just this. This experience of making one thing stand for another is a vital part of learning, since many of the ways in which we describe and represent the world are symbolic. You have only to look around you and observe the written words, hear the sounds, notice the logos and pictures and numerals to realise how important this is. In order to learn to read and write, to talk, to build and draw, to count and measure and to communicate your thoughts and ideas, this knowledge is vital.

Summary

- Abstract learning is difficult for young children, who need a lot of experience of doing things, handling objects, and exploring the physical and social world.
- Children learn best in situations which make 'human sense' to them.
- Children learn best when they have chosen what to do – that is, when they play.
- Through play, children demonstrate all that they know. Observing children at play and paying close attention to what they are actually doing is our best way of understanding what they already know and are interested in.
- Through imaginative play, children begin to understand how to use one thing to represent another – an essential skill in learning how to describe and communicate thoughts and ideas.

It is important to remember that although play is certainly something that children and the young of most species feel impelled to do, its significance in terms of learning is not something that is easily explained or easily understood. Many parents are anxious that when their children play they are wasting their time and not learning. The fears of these parents need to be taken seriously and practitioners need to be able to explain the cognitive benefits of learning to parents to help them appreciate the role of play.

The role of adults

So far we have looked at what the children are doing and not made much mention of what the adults involved with young children do to support and extend their learning. Piaget believed that all that the adults working with young children needed to do was to provide them with an interesting and stimulating environment. This is important, of course. Children do need to encounter new and exciting activities and objects to explore. But some theorists have paid more attention to the role of adults, and it is to their work we turn now. One of the most important people to consider not only the role of adults but that of community was the American researcher Barbara Rogoff. Rogoff spent years looking at children and their learning and development, and she was one of the few people to do this not solely with privileged children in the developed world, but also with children in developing countries such as Guatemala. She believed that children's learning – their cognitive development – was not a solo act but rather an apprenticeship and that this apprenticeship took place through what she called 'guided participation' with others – mainly adults but also peers and older children. These companions, as she called them, support and extend children's understanding of the essential skills and activities needed to become full members of their social group. For children growing up in Guatemala, for example, a skill required by female children is that of carrying water from its source to the home. Little girls copy the actions of their mothers of putting clay pots on their heads and learning how to hold and then balance these.

Vygotsky was not only interested in play. Like Piaget, he saw the child as an active learner, but for him the context in which learning took place was vital. He was interested in how knowledge is passed on from one generation to another, and by definition this implies that people around the child have an important role to play. Vygotsky viewed learning as an essentially social activity. Piaget was more interested in how children acquire knowledge, and his view is thus more focused on the individual child than on the child in society.

Vygotsky believed that children are able to perform at a higher level when they are offered help than if left to struggle on their own. He called the gap between what a child could do unaided and what the child could do with help the 'Zone of Proximal Development'. It is important to understand that this is not something visible to the naked eye. It represents the child's potential.

Think about this:

Dana is pretending to write in the writing area of her nursery (Figure 1.1). The nursery nurse watching her notices that in her pretend writing are some letter shapes, including the D and the A from her name. The adult comments on the fact that Dana already knows how to write some of the letters in her name.

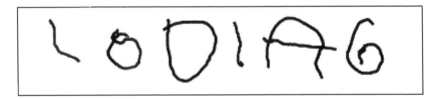

Figure 1.1 Dana's first attempt at writing her name. You can see that the 'D' and 'A' are included in her string of letters.

The next time Dana pretends to write (Figure 1.2), she again makes lots of marks and some letter-like shapes, but this time she says she is writing her name as she writes the D, the A and the N of her name.

Figure 1.2 Dana's second attempt at writing her name. This time you can see that, whilst she still includes a string of letter-like shapes, she has managed to write her name separately.

The adult, by paying careful attention to what Dana was doing, has helped Dana to develop from including some of the letters she knows from her name to writing her name recognisably. The adult has helped the child perform at a higher level, thus bridging the Zone of Proximal Development.

Jerome Bruner, another theorist who has studied the development of young children, describes what the adult has done in the above example as 'scaffolding' the child's learning. A scaffold is something that is erected to help builders gradually construct a building. Once the building is in place, the scaffold is removed. Bruner believed that adults can allow children to take small, supported steps in their learning. When the learning is complete, the support of the adult is no longer needed.

In order to successfully scaffold learning, the adult has to understand both what the child already knows and what the child is paying attention to. The worker in the above example guessed that Dana was interested in writing the letters of her own name. In this case she was right, but there is no guarantee. One way in which you know that you have been correct in your guess is by the child's response. Children quickly let you know when you are way off-beam.

Think about this example in terms of the effectiveness of the adult's intervention.

Harinder, playing in the home corner, brings the playgroup worker a plastic plate on which she has placed some wooden blocks, some bits of plasticine and some beads. 'It's dinner,' she announces, 'sausages and beans and chips.'

'Oh, thank you!' replies the worker. 'How many sausages have you got? Can you count them?'

Harinder picks up the plate and moves away.

The practitioner saw the opportunity to assess the child's knowledge of counting. But counting the sausages was not what Harinder was interested in. Her response was to walk away from the adult. Instead of her learning having been taken forward it was effectively stopped.

So, it is important to try to understand the child's purposes. It is also important to start with what the child already knows. Scaffolding sometimes involves breaking down the task into smaller tasks; sometimes helping the child to become aware of what he or she has achieved; sometimes helping the child sequence what he or she is doing; and sometimes helping the child focus on an aspect of the task which is relevant. These are things that many parents and workers do almost instinctively.

The scaffolding of learning is a skill well worth developing.

Consider these examples and notice what it is the adult does:

Joshua (aged eleven months) puts his empty bottle against the doll's face. His mother says, 'Oh Josh! You are feeding the doll.'

Malindi (aged four years, two months) is retelling the story of 'We're going on a Bear Hunt' from the book and, by mistake, turns over two pages. The nursery worker comments on this and helps her find the right page, so that her retelling of the story continues in the correct order.

Manna (aged four years, seven months) is working with junk materials and announces that she is making a microwave oven for her mother. She has gathered together a large number of boxes and containers and seems to have lost her way. The teacher suggests that she start off by selecting one box for the microwave oven. Once that is done, she guides Manna in selecting the other materials she will need to complete her chosen task.

It should be clear from this that both Bruner and Vygotsky saw the role of adults as crucial. They saw the interaction between the child and adult as one of the most important features of any learning that takes place. When the adult intervenes in the learning situation, the interaction must be sensitive and the adult should not attempt to test the child or to stretch the child too far.

Think about the following examples to assess the effectiveness of intervention:

Louisa is nearly six. She has been working on making a boat out of junk materials. She has been experiencing difficulty in getting the materials to stick together.

'Oh, I need some more glue,' she said and put more glue on and held it tight. 'If it doesn't work this time I'm not going to use it.' As she let go of it, it fell off. She took it and threw it across the table in anger.

'What about using an elastic band?,' I suggested. Louisa agreed and held the form in place while I put an elastic band over it.

'Good, it worked!' she said, looking at the other children. 'That's good, isn't it, using an elastic band?'

(Bragg, in Smidt (ed.) 1998)

Two four-year-olds, Damian and Willy, are playing with magnets. Damian puts the magnets on the table. They attract. He then picks up one of the magnets and a wooden brick. Nothing happens. He tries with the glue pot. Again, nothing happens.

'It won't stick to the brick or the glass, but it sticks to the paper clip,' I said and then added, 'I wonder why?'

Damian tries the sponge and then the metal sharpener. As the sharpener moves across the table towards the magnet, Damian begins to laugh.

'That shoots down, look!'

He picks up the spoon.

'Yeah, a spoon'll stick and a knife. Both do stick to the magnet. It's a bit of a funny trick.'

I then said, 'Some things did stick, but some didn't.'

Later the boys are joined by three-year-old Ollie who asks, 'Do hands stick?'

He picks up one of the magnets and holds it against the palm of his hand. Damian responds, 'No.'

'Why?' asks Ollie.

'Because it hasn't got the thing – the magnet thing.'

I repeat his response, 'The magnet thing?'

Damian goes on, 'The bit that sticks.'

(Lanigan, in Smidt (ed.) 1998)

You will have realised that in each example 'I' referred to the adult. You will also notice, in the second example, how the children were learning from one another. Vygotsky emphasised that children learn from one another and that more advanced children often provide models for younger children.

Summary

- Adults have a key role to play in providing an environment which is stimulating and challenging.
- Adults need to understand what children already know and can do in order to help children develop and learn.
- Adults need to pay careful attention to what children are interested in or are paying attention to.

- Adults need to ensure that their intervention is sensitive and focused on the child's interests and not on their own agenda.
- Scaffolding children's learning helps children bridge the gap between what they can do alone and what they can do with help.

The importance of language in learning

You will remember that Piaget believed that the role of the adult was primarily to provide a stimulating and challenging environment in which children could learn. He saw language as a system of symbols for representing the world and as something quite separate from the actions which led to reasoning and the development of logical thinking. He believed that explaining things to small children before they were 'ready' was a waste of time. Using words to help children make sense of situations led to children learning what have been called 'empty procedures'. This view of the adult use of language is held by certain practitioners today who believe in what is called 'heuristic play'. Young children are invited to explore new and interesting objects physically without the verbal intervention of adults. Supporters of this approach believe that this allows children to become deeply immersed in what they are doing and prevents them from being distracted by the adult intervention.

Vygotsky and Bruner, by contrast, both regard language as essential to learning. Much of Bruner's early research related to how adults help children acquire language. For him, language involves much more than just talk. It includes gesture, inflection, intonation, body language and signs. Through the early turn-taking games that most primary caregivers play with their infants (things like 'Peekaboo'), young children begin to use language both to communicate and to understand how language itself works. Young children begin to play with language just as they play with objects in the physical world. This verbal play, according to Bruner, is an essential component of development. You will have gathered already that Bruner also believed that adults, when scaffolding learning, use language to help the child make sense of the situation, to reflect on what he or she already knows and can do and to take the next cognitive step.

Vygotsky paid particular attention to the development of speech and thought. He believed that these had different roots but later come together so that it is almost impossible to separate them out. Can you think without language? Can you talk without thinking? For young children, speech is used at first to communicate, to make and share meanings. Later it becomes a tool of thought. By this he meant that language itself can change the way in which children think and learn.

Vygotsky believed that in the earliest stages of speech, children go through a phase of talking aloud to themselves, explaining and describing what they are doing. This 'inner speech' serves to help children plan, control, recall and predict. You may have encountered young children's monologues and wondered what they were doing and why. As children get older, this 'inner speech' becomes more abbreviated. Children no longer have to describe to themselves every step of what they are doing. The 'inner speech' becomes internalised as children become aware of what they are thinking. Children need to be aware of what they are thinking in order to learn.

This self-awareness comes partly through the internalisation of inner speech, but also through interactions with others. Adults often reflect back to children what they have said or done, and in doing this they help children become aware of their own achievements. You can find evidence of this in the magnets example in the previous section. Where the adult draws the child's attention to something the child has done, the adult helps fill the gap between what the child can do alone and what the child can do with help – the Zone of Proximal Development. In other words, the adult allows the child to make conscious what he or she already knows and can do.

So, children need both 'inner speech' and social speech (talking to and with others). Vygotsky believed that children learn first by trying to discover what something is or what it does through observing an experienced learner and learning from that. Then the child tries unaided, using 'inner speech' to explain the process. Learning is consolidated when the child internalises the concept.

Children encounter spoken language in all the activities they engage in at home. This applies to all children, whatever their backgrounds, cultures or languages. Parents, other family members, friends and carers use language as a normal part of everyday life. Every situation you can think of is bathed in language: cooking the supper, going to the bus, walking to the shops, digging in the garden, and so on. Parents know what their children are interested in and they know what their children already know and what they can do, and so they are tuned into their children's needs, interests and desires. The language within the home becomes a genuine dialogue, with the parent sometimes listening to the child and the child sometimes listening to the parent.

In 1984, Tizard and Hughes studied the language used by the parents of young children and contrasted it with the language used by teachers once children started at school or nursery. There had previously been the notion that working-class parents tended to use an inferior form of language at home with their children, a form of language that did not allow the children to predict, to solve problems and to move away from the here and now in their thinking. The work of Tizard and Hughes (and a subsequent study by Gordon Wells (1987)) disproved this and showed that all parents, whatever their socioeconomic level, use language in order to make and share meaning and they thus enable their children to acquire language, which allows them to think, to learn, to talk and to solve problems.

The failure of many poorer children in the school system cannot, then, be blamed on the language used within the home. What Tizard and Hughes found was that once children started school or nursery, the language used by the adults was very different. Instead of engaging in genuine dialogue around life-like problems and situations, adults in schools tended to subtly test children, often trying to get the child to give the correct answer to questions.

Think about these two examples to see how the language of home and school can be different and have a negative impact on the child.

At home, three-year-old Mpo is waiting for her tea with her sister Zinzi. Their mother slices and butters bread and spreads Marmite on it.

'Here, girls,' she says as she brings the sandwiches to the table. 'I've cut each slice in half so you can have two each.'

'Two for me and two for you,' says Mpo.

'That's four,' says five-year-old Zinzi.

At nursery, Mpo takes a piece of cardboard over to the teacher.

'Can you cut it in half for me?' she asks. 'The scissors are too hard for me.'

The teacher obliges and, handing the two pieces of card back to the child, asks, 'And what have you got?'

Mpo looks baffled. The teacher repeats the question.

'Two?' suggests Mpo hopefully.

'Two what?' persists the teacher, determined that the child use the word 'half' in her response.

'Two . . . cards.'

You will notice that in the second example the child actually requests that the adult cut the card in half. Had the adult been paying proper attention to the child, she would not have had to test the child as she did.

Summary
- Language is vital for learning, although there may well be times when children are so deeply involved in what they are doing that the adult does not need to intervene verbally.
- Children learn from watching experienced learners, by using 'inner speech' and by internalising the concept.
- Children need both 'inner speech' and social speech.
- Language which involves a genuine dialogue and allows the child to be an equal participant is more likely to take learning forward than instructing, questioning and testing.

So what should young children be doing?

We will now turn to the work of someone writing today. Lilian Katz has spent many years considering how young children learn best. She believes that we already know a great deal about how children learn and develop, and that this knowledge should inform the curriculum we offer to young children. In her paper 'What Should Young Children Be Doing?' she draws a distinction between what children can do and what children should do:

> Just because children can do something when they are young does not mean that they should do it. . . . You can make children work for gold stars and tokens and all sorts of rewards, but that doesn't mean you should. What's interesting is that almost anything you get young children to do they appear to be willing to do. They don't appear to be suffering and some of then even look as though they love it.
>
> (1988, p. 29)

For Katz, the developmental question is not just how children learn – because children always learn. Some children learn to lie, some to cheat, some to steal, some to read. The essential question is: what is it that young children should be doing that will best serve their development in the long run?

Katz is not alone in believing that this is a crucial question facing educators and carers alike. Learning is about more than acquiring skills and knowledge: it involves both feelings and attitudes, or what Katz calls 'dispositions'. A disposition can be defined as a habit of mind. You may have the disposition to be friendly or the disposition to be unfriendly. Almost all young children have the disposition to be curious. We have seen how children actively seek to make sense of the world and eagerly explore all new opportunities and experiences. Where children encounter inappropriate learning experiences there is a very real danger that this disposition – to be a learner – will be damaged.

Think about what you consider might be inappropriate learning experiences for young children.

What did you come up with? Theorists like Katz and David Elkind believe that where children encounter formal learning at too young an age they may learn the skills and knowledge required at that point, but their dispositions to be learners may be damaged. Elkind believes that children forced into formal learning too soon become less independent thinkers and tend to become very reliant on adults. They do not develop their abilities to be reflective learners or to be aware of what they can do and what they know. They are dependent on the adults around them to reward their efforts with praise, or gold stars, or whatever system of approval operates in their playgroup or nursery. Such children may lose interest in what it is they are doing (the process), because all the approval they get relates to the end product. They become like little workers on an assembly line, getting through their 'work' as quickly as possible so that they can then go on and do what really matters to them – that is, play. Children in such formal and inappropriate learning situations will not get deeply involved in what they are doing.

Summary
- Learning involves more than acquiring skills and knowledge: it also involves feelings and dispositions.
- What children do affects how they feel about themselves as learners.
- A too formal curriculum introduced at too early an age may result in children showing short-term gains in skills and knowledge, but at the cost of long-term damage to their dispositions to be learners.
- Those working with young children should enable children to get deeply involved in what they are doing and, in interacting with children, should try to concentrate on what the children are doing rather than on any end product.

A last word

In this introductory chapter we have looked briefly at what some of the theorists and researchers have said about how young children learn best. We have established that learning has a precise meaning – the establishment of connections between brain cells – and that this happens most efficiently where children are able to explore their world in as many ways as possible. Children are naturally curious, and when they are encouraged to follow their own interests – that is, to play – they will become deeply involved and may spend a long time exploring something. This in-depth play is what educators are seeking to encourage in the early years.

We have explored the role of adults and seen that it involves not only providing a stimulating and challenging environment, but also interacting sensitively and in a way which is likely to help the child take the next step in learning and development. Interaction will be most supportive where the adult is able to tune in to what it is the child is interested in and in what the child is exploring. We have seen how important the role of language is in learning and how adults can use language to extend learning where they engage in genuine dialogue with children.

We have recognised that young children are very busy trying to make sense of their world. They learn by drawing on what they already know and have experienced, and need many experiences set in familiar and meaningful contexts to help them. In this way they are able to move towards being able to hold images and ideas in their heads and then to cope with the abstract learning that is required of them at school.

Many people believe that the younger you start teaching a child, the better the results will be. You will have encountered parents who eagerly teach their very young children to read and write. As Lilian Katz reminds us, young children are very obliging and will learn anything we teach them. But the consequences of such early formal learning may be negative in the long term. It is important to keep reminding ourselves that children in Britain start formal schooling at an earlier age than in any other developed country. Increasingly, children are starting in the reception class at the age of only four. If these children are going to go on to be successful learners for life, it is important that those working with them bear in mind the important and undisputed findings cited in this chapter.

Chapter 2

How to support and extend the learning of young children

In the first chapter we examined some of the theories and research concerning how young children learn best. We touched on the role of the adult, and in this chapter we will go into that role in more detail. For those of us working with young children, a sound understanding of how children learn is only of use to us if we are able to act on it in the settings we offer to children and their parents. We need to understand what we can do to ensure that children are learning and developing in these settings.

This chapter will be interactive in the sense that you will be given some case studies to read followed by some questions to answer. In this way you are invited to interact with what you read. Do have a go at answering the questions. In many cases you will find there is no right or wrong answer. A lot of what we do in our work is informed guesswork. This applies particularly where we are trying to focus on what the child is doing or what interest the child is following. The only person who knows the answer to this for sure is the child, and we have no way of getting inside the child's head. So, we have to pay close attention, use what we know about how children learn and then make an educated guess.

Think about Maria and try to decide what she is particularly interested in:

Maria (who is four years old) is working in the technology area of her nursery. It is well equipped with both tools and materials. She spends a long time choosing the materials to use. She selects six corks, six milk bottle tops and an egg carton. She sticks a cork in each space of the egg carton and then sticks a bottle top on top of each cork. She takes it over to the nursery nurse and proudly announces that she has made a typewriter.

There are a number of things you might have said. You might have said that Maria was particularly interested in the number 6, or that she was exploring the concept of one-to-one correspondence by putting one thing on top of another. Or you might even have said that she was interested in putting one thing inside of or on top of another, so perhaps she was exploring position.

We have no way of knowing for sure, and the only way in which we can test out our guesses is to make some comment to the child and then assess her reaction. In the real situation from which the example was drawn, the nursery nurse said to Maria, 'I see that you got six corks and six bottle tops and you stuck a cork in each of the six spaces of the egg carton.' Maria beamed at her and immediately decided to make another 'typewriter'. You might like to hazard a guess as to what the child's reaction might have been if the adult, instead of commenting on what she had achieved, had asked her to count the corks or bottle tops.

Setting up the environment

Piaget, you will remember, believed that the essential role of the adult was to provide a stimulating environment in which the child could learn and develop. This is certainly the starting point for good early years provision and one to which you have probably already paid a lot of attention. But you do need to remember that children will learn wherever they are and through whatever is there for them to explore. In the developed world we have access to money and resources, which can certainly create a rich learning environment, and you should do your best to think about what you might provide and how you can ensure that what you provide meets the learning needs of the children.

Not all children are in the fortunate position of Maria in the example above. Many children do not attend well-equipped nurseries, but find themselves in church halls, village halls, draughty rooms, upstairs in someone's front room in a block of flats or in the annex to the local community centre. Not all providers have limitless resources, so what you provide and how you provide it become even more important than they do in the well-funded centre.

There are certain fundamental things all providers should strive to offer. Not all are expensive and many can be found in the homes of parents or be gathered together from jumble sales or car boot sales. If you have parents who are handy and willing to offer their services, they can help by making clothes or home corner furniture or a host of other things. Essentials include books, writing and drawing and painting materials, things to build with, sand and water, and things to encourage domestic and imaginative play.

Ideally, your setting should strive to organise the materials, toys and equipment in such a way that children can make their own choices and be independent in their play. Not only does this fit well with what we have learned about how young children learn but also it releases you for more vital things than finding the scissors or getting the puzzle out of a cupboard. Try to find low storage units and organise your equipment into these. There are many produced by educational suppliers, but these are often expensive. Cheaper ways are just as good: things like baskets or plastic storage tubs. It is also a

good idea both organisationally and educationally to make sure that each basket or tub is labelled with both word and picture. Doing this helps children know where to find and put things and introduces children to the written word in a meaningful context.

Case study 1
We went out and bought a set of plastic containers and then invited the children to help us sort the toys out. They put Lego in one, the train set in another, the farm animals in a third, and so on. I then sat with the children and wrote labels for the containers. The children were really interested in what I was doing and I noticed that they started to write their own labels over the next few days. Then I asked them to help me cut out pictures of the objects and stick these on to the containers next to the names. Some children wanted to draw pictures of the toys and so some labels have a word, a photograph and a child's drawing. We thought it was going to be absolute chaos the first time we set the containers out on the floor in the morning before the children arrived – and it was. But that only lasted for one or two mornings. After that the children settled down. I guess they realised that this was how things were going to have to be every day, so they didn't have to rush from one container to another. Now they are much more able to choose what to do, and often a child will come in, go straight to one container and spend the whole morning playing with great concentration. The other really good thing that has happened is that the children get much more involved in tidying up now. It is like a game for them and they are getting better and better at sorting things out.

Having organised your resources, it is time to think about how to offer children learning activities in familiar and meaningful contexts. You will remember how important it is for young children to be able to build on their previous experience and to see the point of what they are doing. Situations drawn from children's lives can easily be set up in your group and will offer children important learning activities as they play. The most obvious of these is some sort of area where domestic play can take place – in other words, a home corner. Do remember that the homes children come from will vary and you will want to include in your home corner some artefacts and objects which will be familiar to the children in your group.

Case study 2
Our old home corner was very small and we found that the children were not really playing very well in it. We sat down after nursery one day and had a real go at working out what was going wrong. We decided that the children were bored with the things in there and we noticed that the boys hardly went in there at all and our Turkish children would go in, play for a few seconds and then leave. So, we decided to ask the parents to help out. The Turkish mothers brought in a Turkish coffee pot and some dressing-up clothes. One mother brought in a Turkish newspaper. Then one of the black mothers commented that all our dolls were white, so we went out and bought a black doll. One of the staff thought about bringing in an old tool box and some 'do it yourself' magazines. We got the children to help us rearrange things to make the area bigger. Since then – and that is at least six months ago – the children have been playing in there with much greater concentration and we notice many more children doing things like pretending to read the newspapers or to write messages, and playing many more roles while acting out complex sequences.

It seems obvious that where children encounter a range of materials to play with, their play will become increasingly complex and engrossing. If you have things like knives and forks in your home corner, do try to have complete sets of these – say four knives and four forks. This will help the children in their understanding of numbers and allow them to imitate some of the roles they see their families play at home. Do remember not only to reflect the range of cultures in your group but also to respect them. Not all families use knives and forks, for example. In some cultures, food is eaten using the hands; in others, people use tools such as chopsticks.

In many settings, workers try to extend the opportunity for children to encounter familiar and meaningful situations beyond the home corner by creating another imaginative play area. This could be a launderette, a supermarket, a baby clinic, a garage or any one of a host of other possibilities. A wonderful example of doing this is given by Hall and Robinson (1995), who describe how a teacher took her class to visit a local garage and then set up a garage in the classroom. The teacher was particularly interested in developing children's writing skills, and the children embarked on a number of exciting and unusual writing acts where they did things like filling in forms for planning permission, writing letters, designing posters, etc. Drawing from the meaningful context of the garage, the children were able to explore the many different purposes for which people write in a way that made sense to them.

Summary

- Children need a range of interesting and challenging objects and situations in which to play and learn.
- Children will learn best when the situations they find make sense to them and allow them to draw on what they already know and can do.
- The way in which resources are organised and labelled can encourage children to develop independence and make valid choices.
- The resources should reflect both the cultures and the languages of the children in the group.

Planning your activities

In many nurseries and playgroups the adults tend to offer the basic things like sand and water, construction and home corner play each day, together with a number of 'table-top' activities – things like jigsaw puzzles, cutting and sticking and junk modelling. This type of planning reflects planning without considering the individual needs of the children and sometimes means that the children become fixed in their play and may become bored and troublesome. Let us refer back to some of what we covered in the first chapter and remind ourselves of what Vygotsky called the 'Zone of Proximal Development'. He said that when given help, children can achieve far more than they can unaided. The implication of this is that we need to be aware of what the child can do alone and then help the child to make the next leap in learning.

You cannot, of course, closely study each of 30 children every day to assess their present level and think of what you can do to take each child's learning forward. This would be a physical and intellectual impossibility. What you can do, however, is to select a number of children to observe closely each day, or even to observe one area of your room and take note of how the children play and learn in that area.

Case study 3

At the end of each day the staff gather together for a brief but focused summary of the day's events. In this playgroup each staff member is a key worker for a number of children and it is these children they focus on. Of course they may not focus on each of these children every day, but they keep careful notes to ensure that no child is forgotten or over-looked.

Maria, a parent volunteer, comments that Jordan has been unsettled and weepy and suggests that it may be the presence of the new baby that is upsetting her. The group decide that they will set up a baby clinic in the home corner area and spend a few minutes discussing what materials and equipment they will need and how they will gather this together.

The group leader, Alicia, says she thinks that four-year-old Hamish is on the verge of reading. She observed him retelling the story of 'Not Now Bernard' and actually pointing to the words as he did so. She volunteers to take a group of the older children (those who are inter-ested, and hopefully including Hamish) to make a 'Big Book' version of the story. The children can do the illustrations and she will model the writing by doing it in front of them. She can invite individual children to guess what letter a word starts with or to write words she knows they can write.

Paulette thinks that three-year-old Sukvinder is including Urdu symbols in her 'writing'. She suggests inviting Sukvinder's mother in to sit in the writing corner and maybe write a letter in Urdu. She will make sure that there is writing paper, envelopes and stamps in the writing area.

Alicia says that four-year-old Darren is very interested in circles. He has been drawing them, making circular movements out in the garden and including circles in all his attempts at writing. She wants to put out a lot of circular shapes in the junk modelling area and observe what Darren does with these.

You will see that in this example the adults have been paying close atten-tion to the children in order to decide how to help them in their learning. In the next example you will find the staff focusing more on what they have provided and using this as the basis for planning.

Case study 4

In this nursery, each member of staff takes responsibility for setting up a number of activities and then spends time in them observing the children at play.

Lettie says that she had put a number of plastic containers in the water tray. 'Some of the children were filling them up with water and then pushing them to the bottom of the water tray to try and make them sink. I'm going to put the same containers in the water tomorrow, but I'm also going to include some stones. I want to see if the children try putting the stones in the containers and see what happens.'

Julian says that he read a group of children 'The Jolly Postman' and that they were really interested in the letters. He is going to put writing paper and envelopes out in the writing area and is going to rescue the postbox they had around at Christmas time. The nursery head suggests that he might like to base himself in the writing area and be seen by the children actually writing a letter himself.

Natasha has been observing the home corner and says that she feels that the children are really stuck in their play. They seem to act out the same sequences every day. 'I am going to bring in something new to see if that changes the play,' she says. 'Why don't you set up the home corner in the nursery by putting an old toaster on the table together with some tools from the woodwork area?' suggests the nursery head.

A number of important points have been raised by these examples. In the first place, it is clear that in order to plan for learning and development, you have to pay close attention to what children are doing and what they are interested in. In the second place, it is worth remembering that children do need long periods of time in order to get deeply involved in what they are doing. If you divide up your day into short periods of 'work' and 'play', you make this impossible. Further, children sometimes need to explore something not just over one day, but over several. In the second example you will have noticed that Lettie was not going to put something completely different in the water on the following day. She was going to let the children continue their exploration of whether or not the plastic containers would sink or not, but she was going to add something new to the existing activity. Now, this is a vital point for all nursery workers. Where children are interested in exploring something, adding something new or even taking something away from the activity will offer the children an intellectual challenge and encourage them to further their explorations.

Think about this.

How would the addition of stones to the water tray offer children a cognitive challenge? Or would you just put some completely different things in the water next day?

In Case Study 4 Lettie, possibly without knowing it, is operating the theory of 'Match' devised by McVicker Hunt. He believed that children will be assisted in their learning when they are offered something new in a situation, but he emphasised that the gap between the old and the new must be neither too big nor too small. Where the gap between what the child is exploring and the new situation is too big, children are not able to make the cognitive leap involved. Where the gap is too small, there is no intellectual challenge and the children will not be learning. Lettie believed that the children were exploring whether or not the containers, filled with water, would sink. By offering them stones to put inside the containers she was helping them realise something about weight and buoyancy. Had she decided to remove the plastic containers and just put some stones in the water, she would not have allowed the children to make the link between what they had been doing (filling the containers) and the new activity. The theory of 'Match' is a very useful one for nursery workers and is certainly worth bearing in mind when planning activities.

You will see the link between the theory of 'Match' and the work of Vygotsky. The introduction of the novel object or activity helps the child move from where he or she is now to a higher plane of learning and understanding.

Often, when workers are asked why they have provided an activity for children – something like 'cutting and sticking', for example – they respond by saying things like 'Well, the children really love it'.

Think about this response and decide whether it seems an appropriate or an adequate response.

Children like all sorts of things. They like eating sweets and drinking Coca-Cola and watching television. This does not mean that these things are good for them. As nursery workers, our goals must be to enhance children's learning and development, and all activities should be planned with some valid learning goal in mind. If you are planning a cutting and sticking activity, your reason might be to help develop children's use of fine tools. When you plan your activities on the basis of what you have observed about the children, you will almost inevitably have to have a learning goal in mind.

Summary
- Activities need to be planned to meet the learning needs of children.
- Adults need to pay careful attention to what children are doing in order to take their learning forward.
- Workers need to work as a team in order to share their observations and plan together. This is both efficient and informative. Sharing information and planning together brings about an element of continuity and a sense of shared values.
- Introducing something new (either by bringing in a novel object or by removing something) can take learning forward as long as the gap between the old and the new is carefully matched.
- Children need extended periods of time in which to explore. This allows them to follow their own interests and solve the problems they set themselves in their play.
- The best planning does not mean offering something different every day. Children may need to do the same things over and over again.

Intervening and interacting

> It is a sunny Monday morning and all the children are out in the garden area. Some are playing in the sandpit, some are on the climbing frames, and some are racing round on bikes and trikes. The adult who is 'on duty' is sitting on a chair where she has a good view of all the activities. She is drinking a cup of tea and, every so often, yells a warning. Occasionally children come over to her to be comforted or to ask for something. When asked what her role is, she confidently replies that she is there in order to ensure that the children play safely. Her role is that of supervisor.

It is obvious that children's safety must be a prime concern and workers must do everything they can to ensure this. But since nurseries are about learning and development, the role of the adult is much more important than merely one of supervision. It is about more, even, than ensuring that you have provided a stimulating and challenging environment with many meaningful activities which you have planned according to what you have observed about children's existing knowledge and current interests.

From birth, children are involved in interactive acts with adults and others. Wells (1987) believes that children are impelled to interact, especially through speech, because of their urge to communicate their desires and needs more explicitly. Maxwell (1996) believes that this urge extends to a need to be close, to experience warmth and acceptance.

For Wells, interaction is like the act of throwing a ball to a small child:

> First ensure the child is ready with arms cupped to catch the ball, throw gently and accurately so that it lands squarely in the child's arms. When it is the child's turn to throw, the adult must be prepared to run wherever the ball goes.
>
> (1986, p. 50)

You will recognise in this example just how much responsibility for an effective interaction rests with the adult as the more experienced partner in the reciprocal exchange. Wells goes on to say:

> [I]f the adult and child are to succeed in elaborating a shared meaning over a number of turns the adult has to make the effort to understand the child's intended meaning and to extend it in terms that the child can understand.
>
> (1986, p. 17)

This is the essence of effective interaction. Let us try to draw out the meaning more clearly. By referring to 'shared meaning', Wells is talking about both parties – adult and child – paying attention to the same thing. The adult has to pay close attention to what it is the child is exploring in order that his or her interaction with the child can be focused on that. Adults sometimes have their own agenda in mind and when working with a child take the opportunity to teach the child something – the names of colours, numbers, shapes, for example. But the child may be paying attention to something much more complex, and if the adult is wrong in his or her guess about the child's focus of attention, the interaction breaks down.

Think about the following examples and in each case say first what you believe the child is paying attention to and then suggest what you might do or say. Do remember that there are no right or wrong answers.

- Jonas has been playing in the construction area every day for well over a week. Each time he constructs something he pays a great deal of attention to ensuring that his construction is symmetrical.

- You notice that Rehana has taken a long strip of paper from the writing area and has gone over to the children's coat pegs and is laboriously copying each child's name in a list on this piece of paper.

- You have been doing some number songs with a group of children and you notice that three-year-old Bernie knows all the words and, what is more, uses her fingers when she is counting down.

How did you get on with doing this? You might like to compare your responses with some gathered from workers in the area:

- In the case of Jonas and his symmetrical buildings, one nursery worker said, 'I would certainly use the word "symmetrical" in my response. I would say something like "My goodness, Jonas. Every time you make something it is the same on both sides. We call that symmetrical." I might then bring a mirror into the construction area and see what he makes of that. Or I could put out some folded paper and see if he is interested in something like "blot" paintings.'

- In the case of Rehana making a list of names, one nursery nurse said, 'I would assume (perhaps wrongly) that Rehana was making a register. She sees us walking round each morning with a register ticking off names. So assuming she is drawing on this experience I might try and just put in words what I think she is doing. I'd say, "You're making a register, Rehana, just like the one I use in the mornings to check that the children are here." By doing this I would validate what she is doing and help her become conscious of what she already knows. If I noticed that she could actually recognise some of the names (and I am pretty sure she could), I might get her to help me check the register the next day. Or I could put out an empty register book and see what she does with that. In the longer term I would perhaps make a book for her in which we could include the names she recognises – like a song the children know: something like "Poor Jenny sits a-weeping".'

- In the case of three-year-old Bernie and her knowledge of numbers, one playgroup worker said, 'I would comment on what she already knows per-haps by saying something like "You know all the words of the songs, Bernie, and you are using your fingers to count down. That's what I do, isn't it? And I sometimes use the children as well." I just want to draw her attention to her achievements. I would carry on doing number songs and maybe make her a book of one of them. She could help by doing the drawings or by stick-ing things in.'

If you think about how you interact with other people – your friends or colleagues or family – you will realise that all your interactions involve relat-ing about something. It may be about who is going to set up the garden equipment in the morning or about what film you are going to see or about who is collecting the children from school. Bruner's research in 1980 showed that most of the interactions between teachers and children in schools focused on managerial issues and were primarily concerned with teachers responding to children's achievements with comments like 'Good boy!' or 'Well done!' Bruner suggests that those involved with children would do better to try to tune into what children are doing in more supportive ways. With older children, interactions might involve discussing with children aspects of the task in which they have been involved. Whatever the inter-action, the response of the adult gives the child some idea of the adult's views of the child, of learning, of the world. In other words, interactions are about more than the child's behaviour or performance: they are part of the process of exchanging views and sharing meanings.

Summary
- Children learn through interaction with more experienced learners – either older children or adults.
- Interaction involves the sharing of meaning and requires the adult to pay close attention to the child's concerns in order that the child can be helped to make the next step.
- The role that adults play is complex, involving them in planning activities, talking to children, listening to children, observing children, thinking about what the children are doing, interacting.
- Adults should play a role that is more than merely supervising children's play.
- Children's learning can be scaffolded by the adult reflecting back to the child what the child already knows and can do. This helps the child become conscious of his or her own achievements.

Guided participation

Barbara Rogoff (1990) is an American researcher who has done some interest-ing work on the role of adults in extending the learning of young children. She clearly builds on much of the work of Vygotsky and Bruner but takes a broader sociocultural view, reflecting her own research with different com-munities. She sees that all children are born into a world where they quickly become tied into a system of relationships with others – their caregivers, their siblings, their peers, and so on. These more mature learners are already involved with all the activities of their culture and they induct the new infant into these. It is a two-way collaborative process, with the children wanting to participate and to increase their understanding and the adult seek-ing to develop shared understanding.

It is quite difficult to see how this is different from scaffolding. Rogoff argues that this guided participation (as she calls it) is something done in all societies and that it does not involve direct teaching and often not even contact or conversation. What happens is that children are involved in the routines and rituals of daily life, and through this, alongside the more experienced learners, come to be part of a shared culture. She argues that guided participation appears throughout the world.

> Caregivers and children make arrangements for children's activities and revise children's responsibilities as they gain skill and knowledge. These arrangements and adjustments facilitate children's extension of their existing knowledge to encompass new situations. With the guidance of those around them, children participate in cultural activities that socialize them in skilled roles.
>
> (Rogoff 1990, p. 111)

Think about some of the examples she cites and consider how to understand and support the learning of younger children.

Maria is reading 'Ten in the Bed' with twenty-month-old Efraim. He joins in to chant some numbers, showing that he has appropriated familiar routines involving counting.

Valerie, who is not yet two, picks up her table mat to show the family, but she holds it face down. Her parents do not comment but her four-year-old sister gently tells her that it is upside down. Valerie looks down at the mat and turns it round so that it faces her family.

Children in a South African nursery class routinely fasten their dolls to their backs using strips of cloth.

An eleven-month-old child in Zaire cuts a fruit with a machete, watched by a relative.

Can you see from these examples how both adults and other children induct children into the routines and rituals of their culture? Can you also see how important it is for those working with young children to have some knowledge of and sensitivity to the similarities and variations within and between cultural practices?

It is clear that the role of the adult in supporting and extending children's learning is a complex one. Adults working with young children need to be knowledgeable about how young children learn best and to be sensitive in their interactions with both children and their carers. A recent trend in some countries of calling all those who work with young children 'facilitators' is concerning. The use of this term implies that the role is limited to facilitating learning, and, as we have seen in this chapter, it is about much more than that. As an adult working with young children, you will often be facilitating their learning, but you will also be planning for it, monitoring it, intervening in it to take learning forward. You will be listening, watching, considering, taking notes and making decisions based on your own knowledge of child development and of individual children. The vital role of the adult will be returned to time and again throughout this book.

Summary
- The role of adults is a complex one and adults need to know something about what is thought about how young children learn best.
- Adults need to be sensitive and intervene in ways which do not distract the child from his or her purposes.
- Taking notice of what children are interested in allows for planning to take learning forward in ways that will interest the child.
- Matching what is offered next to what the child has done needs to be carefully considered, and small supportive steps will scaffold learning, allowing the child to move from dependence to independence.

Chapter 3

The new Childcare Bill

Since the previous edition of this book was published there have been – and continue to be – many initiatives regarding the care and education of children under the age of six. We have seen a new document relating to the care and education of children from birth to the age of three (which we discuss in detail later in this chapter) as well as the publication of the significant document *Every Child Matters* and a revised Children Act 2004. Arising out of all this will be the Childcare Bill, which is due to be published before the end of 2006, resulting in what will be called the Early Years Foundation Stage – due to be introduced in 2008 and effectively merging Birth to Three, the Foundation Stage and elements of the National Standards for under-eights day care and childminding. This will be compulsory for all those currently registered with OFSTED as well as for independent, maintained and non-maintained settings catering for children under the age of three. The new regulations will apply to all children from birth until 31 August following any child's fifth birthday. It will have the same legal status as the Foundation Stage currently has under the National Curriculum and will remove the Foundation Stage from the National Curriculum.

The Early Years Foundation Stage will start with six areas of learning and development. These are:

- personal, social and emotional development;
- communication, language and literacy;
- problem-solving, reasoning and numeracy;
- knowledge and understanding of the world;
- physical development; and
- creative development.

You will see that there are few changes in the six learning areas, but those there are, are significant. Mathematics, for example, currently in the Foundation Stage, is to be replaced with the more relevant and meaningful problem-solving, reasoning and numeracy. The new documents will specify early learning goals, educational programmes and assessment arrangements, and it is encouraging to read that these are going to be largely based on the observations adults make of children at play. Another change is the introduction of aspects of welfare – things like the qualifications and training of the adults, the suitability of the premises and resources, how complaints are dealt with and how records are kept. In a press release called 'Direction of Travel' (December 2005) we are reminded that the current Foundation Stage was built on research into early childhood provision – specifically the Effective Provision of Pre-school Education (EPPE) – a longitudinal study – and Researching Pedagogy in the Early Years (REPEY). Birth to Three was based on a reading of relevant literature and publications, including a project carried out by Professor Edward Melhuish in June 2004 for the Daycare Trust. This showed that three aspects of interaction between children and carers were key: affection, responsiveness and communication.

The new document will highlight the importance of children learning through self-chosen activities – that is, through play – and will advocate that there is a sensible balance between child- and adult-initiated activities. The starting point for all provision will be the five outcomes detailed in *Every Child Matters* and the Children Act (2004):

- Be healthy.
- Stay safe.
- Enjoy and achieve.
- Make a positive contribution.
- Achieve economic well-being.

Settings will use the four aspects of *Birth to Three Matters*, work towards the early learning goals and look ahead to the five aspects outlined above. The fourteen national standards may also apply. It is a far-reaching proposal, making some needed changes and bringing together currently separate strands into one document and one legal framework.

The early years curriculum I: *Birth to Three Matters*

Since 1997 there have been a number of initiatives regarding the care and education of young children, including very young children. One of the most important things to happen was the bringing together of childcare and education and a recognition that what happens to children in their earliest years may be critical to their subsequent development.

Increasingly, women who are mothers want or need to return to work after the birth of their children. There is still a view in the United Kingdom that these women are 'bad' mothers, who put their careers or their financial security before the well-being of their children. There is also a general and lingering suspicion of childcare away from the home, despite a substantial body of evidence highlighting the benefits of children being with other children and other adults. Dahlberg *et al.* (2004), in the most recent edition of their book looking at quality in early childhood provision, talk, deliberately, of early childhood institutions rather than of early childhood services. They point out that a service implies a giver and a taker, a buyer and a seller. This is the language of the market. Talking of institutions, they argue, takes the discussion into a more public arena where aspects of culture and society, fairness and equity, may be discussed.

Despite the bringing together of care and education, parents are still faced with a plethora of perplexing choices when making decisions about what to do with their young children. The wealthy might employ a nanny or an au pair, or send their child to a private nursery. Some might opt for playgroups, where parents often play a role. Many will try to get their children into the nursery school if there is one in their area and if there is a space. These are often like gold dust! Many will send their children to day care centres and more and more will select children's centres offering all-day provision.

Think about these words:

Nursery, crèche, childcare centre, daghem, *asilo nido* (which means 'nest'), nursery school, nursery class, kindergarten, *école maternelle, scuola d'infanzia,* children's centres, wrap-around care, maintained schools, private schools, special schools, independent schools, playgroups

And these:

Teacher, teaching assistant, nursery nurse, childcare worker, practitioner, educationalist, carer, pedagogue, volunteer, helper, centre manager, Sure Start manager, childminder, nanny, au pair

And these:

Montessori, Reggio Emilia, High Scope, Sure Start, Steiner, schemas, Te Whaariki, Foundation Stage, *Birth to Three Matters, Every Child Matters*

Are you confused? Not surprising, really. These words have been taken out of several current and popular books on early childhood education and care, and it is no wonder that those working with children or thinking about their learning and development feel that they are walking through treacle. We are not going to unpick all these terms now, because there is not the space. You have been asked to think about them purely to get a sense of the complexity of the field.

In 1997 the UK government decided that the time was ripe for developing what it called a framework to support those working with children from birth to the age of three. Already in place was the Curriculum Guidance for the Foundation Stage, which applies to children from the age of three to the age of five-plus. (We will turn our attention to that in the next chapter.) The resulting document was called *Birth to Three Matters* (Department for Education and Skills 2004b), a title which holds the promise of a recognition of something we all know. In the foreword to the document, Baroness Ashton tells us that the publication of the document constitutes

> a milestone in recognising and valuing our youngest children and the contribution made to their growth and development by the adults who work with them. It raises the status of work with this important age group and marks our commitment to supporting quality and effective practice with children from birth to three.

The document was, in fact, developed by practitioners and its purpose was to offer support, guidance, information and challenge for all those working with these young children. Here are the fundamental *purposes* of *Birth to Three Matters*. You might want to comment on them. Try picking out what appear to you to be key words or phrases.

- values and celebrates babies and children;
- recognises their individuality, efforts and achievements;
- recognises that all children have, from birth, a need to develop, learning through interaction with people and exploration of the world around them. For some children, this development may be at risk because of difficulties with communication and interaction, or cognition and learning; or with behaviour, emotional and social development or sensory and physical development;
- recognises the 'holistic' nature of development and learning;
- acknowledges, values and supports the adults who work with babies and young children;
- provides opportunities for reflection on practice;
- informs and develops practice whilst acknowledging that working with babies and children is a complex, challenging and demanding task and that often there are no easy answers.

Perhaps, like me, you found unpicking the purposes of this document quite difficult. It is difficult to see how a purpose which talks of valuing adults without talking about their pay and conditions makes a great deal of sense. Those working as childcare workers know that their training, status and conditions do not yet match these laudable aims.

The underpinning principles

The document lists a set of principles which have been developed by people from a number of different backgrounds, with different experiences. Included are leading childcare writers, experts and practitioners and some representative organisations. Each of the principles is listed below and then examined in light of what is known and believed about how children learn and develop in these, the earliest years.

- *Parents and families are central to the well-being of the child.* No one could question that parents and families are central to the child's well-being – but for some of the world's children, life is less simple. It is a fact that there are children without parents and families, and children whose support networks are complex webs of community, peer and family members. These children are just as capable of learning and developing as children in secure families as long as they are able to establish long-term, trusting and respectful relationships with others.
- *Relations with other people (both adults and children) are of crucial importance in a child's life.* Loris Malaguzzi, the founder of the Reggio Emilia pre-school programmes, believed in an education based on relationships. These are, by necessity, complex and diverse, and operate between children, and between children and adults – and, of course, between the adults who work with the children. In centre-based settings, staff can work together as a group and in doing this can offer one another mutual support, a dialogue about the children and the possibility of documenting what they do. In some sense these groups model the forms of discussion groups found in civil society.
- *A relationship with a key person at home and in the setting is essential to the young child's well-being.* Once children start school they may have one class teacher, but the ratios are rather too large for this to count as a relationship with one key person. The emphasis on key people working with the youngest children is a positive one and one that might well be routinely extended to those in nursery and reception classes.
- *Babies and young children are social beings; they are competent learners from birth.* Babies are born into a social world. They are surrounded by people – children and adults – and from the moment of birth they are engaged in dialogues and exchanges with these others. Through their interactions with others, babies move from dependence to independence; they acquire their first language(s) and learn to feed and dress themselves. They develop their own sense of self and build self-esteem and confidence. At the same time they are curious and actively seeking to understand every aspect of their physical, social and emotional worlds. No one has to give babies lessons in how to speak, or in how to try things out or in how to think.

These are things that human infants seem hard-wired to do through their interactions.

- *Learning is a shared process and children learn most effectively when, with the support of a knowledgeable and trusted adult, they are actively involved and interested.* There are some key words in this principle – shared, support, actively involved and interested. Rogoff, whose work I have mentioned, has shown how children in the developed and the developing worlds learn through guided participation – alongside expert members of their community. The children are active in their watching and listening and hence in their learning. And they are interested because what they are learning is relevant, even essential, to their communities and their lives. It is worth remembering this point when we come to considering what happens to children when they go into the Foundation Stage.

- *Caring adults count more than resources and equipment.* This principle spells out what has been mentioned earlier – that a learning environment does not have to be one rich in resources. It adds more weight to the notion of education being something built on relationships.

- *Children learn when they are given appropriate responsibility, allowed to make errors, choices and decisions, and respected as autonomous and competent learners.* This is another important point and one worth remembering throughout your reading of this book. Children who are allowed to play can make choices and errors and decisions, and in our culture it is common for play by very young children to be accepted and valued. We hear people talking about 'play being a child's work'. Sadly, this often changes when children reach the age of statutory education, at which stage they are expected to cope with abstract learning – learning which does not allow them to build on their prior experience. When children play at this stage it is often regarded as time-wasting and it is talked of as 'just playing'.

- *Children learn by doing rather than by being told.* Anyone who has tried to teach a young child something by telling them what to do or not to do knows how useless this is. Children have to do things, get things wrong, work out the pattern, try again, get things wrong again, try again, and so on. Children learn through doing and thinking about what they do. Doing involves a considerable amount of thinking or cognition.

- *Young children are vulnerable. They learn to be independent by having someone they can depend on.* This is a principle which is difficult to analyse. Some young children are more vulnerable than others, and many older children – and even adults – are vulnerable. It is probably true that children learn to be independent sometimes by having people to depend on, but the reality – particularly in the developing world – is that many children become independent purely because they have to. Life demands it.

Think about what you have read so far and decide whether you feel this represents an acceptable view of babies and young children and how they learn and develop.

It is clear that this is a view of babies and children that sees them as competent learners, learning through their own active search for meaning and through the interactions they form with adults and with other children. It is a view that does not suggest that children with access only to resources other than people and experiences will not learn. It is what we might call a humane, positive and optimistic view of young children and their learning. Based on this, the Framework (i.e. *Birth to Three Matters*) starts with the child and does not talk of subjects, learning areas or clear curriculum headings. Instead it talks of four *Aspects* which are said to celebrate the skill and competence of babies and young children and to consider the links between learning and growth and the development and the environments in which young children and babies are cared for and educated. The four Aspects are as follows:

- A Strong Child;
- A Skilful Communicator;
- A Competent Learner; and
- A Healthy Child.

Each of these is divided into four *Components*, as will be illustrated in what follows. Accompanying the Framework is a set of cards which are designed to help those working with babies and toddlers know what to do. Although there are some good suggestions on these cards, a word of warning: despite all the words to the contrary and advice about thinking of meeting diverse needs (meaning that you think of each child as an individual), the whole is still based on very Western notions of what constitutes development, and there is a tendency to assume that children will develop in a linear fashion through clear age-related phases. Most experts nowadays feel that this is not a very useful way of thinking about development across cultures and across ways of reading children.

A Strong Child

The idea of the strong child runs through the Framework, and the aim for all children is that they should become strong, able, confident and self-assured. The components which practitioners will want to work through include the following:

Me, myself and I

This is all about helping children to develop a sense of themselves (their self-concept) and a sense of their own abilities and capabilities. It is also about helping children know that they are separate and different from others and to develop a sense of their own personal characteristics and preferences. Finally, it is about helping children discover what they can do.

Think about these small vignettes. The first two are drawn from diaries of their own children's development made by parents and cited in Karmiloff-Smith (1994):

Amy (eight and a half months): Amy has taken a leap forward in social skills. When she sees herself in a mirror she really is all smiles. She will even look at herself lovingly in the dark glass of the oven doors and sometimes touches her image too. (p. 214)

Sorsha (fifteen and a half months): Sorsha met a friend in the park today, a little girl called Abbi aged twenty months, and she wanted to copy everything she was doing, stamping her feet, going on the roundabout, going on the swings, etc. (p. 217)

Adrian (aged three) told his mother that his favourite fruit was hard-boiled eggs.

When Kirsten fell and cut her knee, her friend Natalya cried too. Both girls were aged two. The nursery worker made a note of the fact because it was the first time she had observed Natalya being able to take on the feelings of someone else.

Being acknowledged and affirmed

Like the previous component, this is aimed at building children's sense of self and building confidence. Its primary focus is on emotional development and helping children explore emotional boundaries safely. It is very much to do with helping children establish strong relationships in order to learn about their role in the lives of others.

Think about these examples:

Kareem (aged two) arrives in the morning unwilling to part from his mum. As he starts to cry, his key worker picks him up, cuddles him and says, 'Oh, my little friend Kareem. I really need you to help me this morning. You are my best early-morning helper, aren't you?

Caspar (aged two), when told he cannot have a sweet before he has his tea, throws himself to the floor and throws a typical terrible twos tantrum! His mum says, 'It won't help, Cas. Food first and then a sweet. Just like yesterday and the day before and the day before that.'

Developing self-assurance

Through strong and close relationships the young child gains confidence about his or her relationships with others and confidence in what he or she can do. In this way the child begins or continues to feel valued and supported and to recognise and appreciate the things that he or she can do.

Think about these examples:

'I can build a tower right up to the 'ky,' announced three-year-old Nicola when she came into the nursery one morning. 'Really?' responded the nursery nurse. 'Do you want me to get the ladder out for you?'

'Help me,' pleaded two-year-old Dana, pointing to the climbing frame. 'I too scared.'

A sense of belonging

Children's gaining a sense of belonging refers to their acquiring both social confidence and competence so that they can enjoy close contact: develop trust, contributing as an individual and as part of a group and having a clear role and identity within a group.

A Skilful Communicator

It will come as no surprise that communication is highlighted as an Aspect. In the earliest years of life children achieve the almost miraculous task of acquiring their first language(s), and they do this without having to have lessons in language. Quite how this takes place is still not clearly understood, although we do know that the learning is social; that the child is active and often the initiator of exchanges; that the child seeks to find and convey meaning; and that there is a growing body of evidence to show that even very young children come to understand the intentions of others.

Being together

'Being together' refers to what takes place in the earliest years and beyond to enable the child to become a social person and an effective communicator. Much of this relates to how children get attention, share attention with others and make contact, and has much to do with building strong relations. It is about having dialogues and conversations, listening and responding, paying attention to a range of signs and symbols, finding a voice and, crucially, not only sharing meaning but making meaning.

Think about the examples below in terms of how the children communicate:

Evi, working in a children's centre, noticed that when eleven-month-old Uri wants something he stares fixedly at it. Yesterday she thought he wanted a ball that was in the fruit bowl. When she gave it to him he threw it to the floor and returned to eye pointing. Eventually she discovered that what he wanted was a banana.

Boris points at everything. He seems to have found that when he points, the adult with him names the thing he is pointing at. This is, for him, a very satisfactory game.

Olya (nineteen months), looking at a picture book, saw a picture of a cat and then got up, took hold of the childminder's hand and took her to find her cat.

Lucinda is two, and for her second birthday she got a set of toy vehicles. Initially she called them all cars but now they come in two categories: cars and lorries.

Finding a voice

The 'finding a voice' component refers to how young children become both confident and competent language users. It is important to remember that, although *Birth to Three Matters* does not specifically say so, this refers to whatever language it is that is used primarily in the child's home. Those spending time with the child will support and respect the efforts the child makes to explore, play with the sounds of language, experiment with the rules of language, label and use language to express feelings – laughing, shouting, and crying. With time, children will start to be able to use spoken language to describe, question, represent and predict, to share their thoughts and feelings and ideas.

Think about these examples:

Eight-month-old Sarah lies in her cot and makes noises. She seems to be making the sounds of speech with lots of syllables which she joins together, and clear intonation patterns. So sometimes it sounds like a question and sometimes like a statement and sometimes a very loud and angry shout!

When Sam was a baby she invented words: a cushion was a *bakpi* and sweets were *nunus*. Her parents always understood what she was talking about because she always used the same 'words' for the same objects.

Listening and responding

'Listening and responding' refers to how children listen and respond in appropriate ways to the sounds and the gestures and the meanings of others. It involves listening and paying attention to what others are saying, and responding perhaps seriously or perhaps playfully. It is very concerned with enjoying and sharing stories read and told, songs and rhymes and games and finger plays. It means taking part in prediction games and games with patterned language, and it means learning about words and meanings – although not in the sense of learning anything about grammar or anything other than what takes place in the normal and meaningful exchanges of the day.

Think about the small examples that follow:

Alexandra (twenty-three months), listening to a conversation in Harrods, overheard a man saying to his companion, 'That's all I hear: I want, I want, I want!' Then this little voice piped up 'I want, I want, I want.' (Karmiloff-Smith 1994, p. 160)

Playing the classic peekaboo game, Alex waits, with his breath held, till his father gets to the point in the game where there is a loud clap. He loves this game and is easily able to predict what will happen next. On one occasion, instead of giving the loud clap, his father whispered and Alex dissolved in floods of tears!

'Once upon a time I saw a worm in my garden and it wiggled off. And then it lived happily ever after.' (Story told by three-year-old Ahmed)

Making meaning

'Making meaning' is at the heart of being a skilful and effective communicator and lays the foundations for much that is to come. Primarily it is about understanding the meanings or the intentions, the words and the actions of others and about being understood by others. It involves such vital things as making choices, influencing others and negotiating.

Think about these examples:

A thirty-month-old child here is exploring the meaning of forbidden objects in a discussion with a sibling.

SIBLING: You're not allowed to put knives in your face.
CHILD: Just you?
SIBLING: No. Not me.
CHILD: Glynis?
SIBLING: Not anybody. (Dunn 1988, p. 135)

In another example, Judy Dunn gives us a twenty-eight-month-old child who is trying to understand the fear shown by the mother when a dead mouse has been found.

CHILD: What's that frighten you, Mum?
MOTHER: Nothing . . .
CHILD: What is it? What's that down there, Mummy? That frighten you? (Ibid., p. 137)

The exchange goes on like this over several turns as the child really struggles to make sense of this situation.

A Competent Learner

For decades it has been recognised that babies are not born as blank slates waiting for life to write its plan on them. Rather, from birth (and some suggest even while still in the womb), human infants seek to recognise and analyse the patterned nature of events in the world. Among the earliest things the child sees are human faces, and evidence suggests that very young infants respond to a face-like shape with an array of marks on it that resemble the face: two shapes like eyes, one vertical shape below and in the middle and below that a horizontal shape. By 'respond', researchers mean 'spend time looking at'. It follows that when they see things that do not look like human faces they notice the differences. They develop preferences – likes and dislikes – and they learn to discriminate between one thing and another. All of this involves extremely complex analyses and understandings.

Making connections

'Making connections' is what happens as children explore the world using their senses and movement. Through this they find out about their own world, described by where they live, who lives with them or interacts with them and what is in that environment. So, from the earliest days human infants are finding out about the physical, the social and the emotional worlds they inhabit. Through their explorations and their play they begin to identify and make patterns, and in doing so they compare, categorise and classify.

Think what these examples illustrate:

Ten-month-old Tahiba explores new objects by putting them in her mouth, shaking them, pulling them and swinging them.

Nine-month-old Julio will search for an object that has been hidden. When his mother tried to hide a bottle of water under a towel, he kept lifting up the towel and shrieking with glee when he found the bottle.

Sixteen-month-old Mpho loves to open all the cupboards in the kitchen, take out all the tins of goods, put them in her wooden trolley and take them over to the sink. Then she unpacks them into the sink, back into the trolley and back to the cupboard. She can do this for hours.

Twenty-eight-month-old Cameron took a chair over to the shelves where a book he wanted was stacked. He climbed up on the chair in order to reach the book.

Joseph, playing with small world toys, selected all the animals and put them in one box. Then he put all the grey animals in one pile, all the white animals in another and the rest he left behind.

Being imaginative

'Being imaginative' is another hugely significant component, illustrating how important it is for young children to explore the world in different ways and to create worlds of their own. It involves children in imitating, copying, exploring, representing, re-enacting and pretending. Through pretence, children are able to safely explore difficult or dangerous emotions and situations. As children explore the world through their senses and movement they begin to be able to make mental images of what they experience, and these mental images can later be called upon in the absence of real objects or events. This explains a great deal about why children need enormous experience of being able to play and explore and represent and re-represent. It is primarily through this that children are later able to handle abstract concepts.

Think what children might be exploring through their imaginative play:

When the telephone rings, twenty-three-month-old Harriet immediately picks up her toy telephone and says, 'Hello.' She continues to talk while her mother is on the phone and only stops talking when her mother says goodbye.

Mika is thirty months old. She dresses up in scarves from the dressing up box; one day she is a princess and one day a mummy and one day a teacher and very often the baby. One of the nursery workers has noticed that the princess unfailingly tells the other children what to do, the mummy is often angry and the baby always cries a lot.

In the nursery a computer keyboard is always available. Two children, both aged about two and a half, are arguing about who is better at typing. Each fiercely punches the keyboard and claims she has 'done better writing' than her friend.

Being creative

Closely related to 'being imaginative' is 'being creative'. This component talks about the child exploring and discovering the world using different sounds, other media and movement. It mentions being resourceful. In essence, this relates to what Loris Malaguzzi famously called 'the hundred languages of children', by which he meant the many different ways in which children could explore and represent their ideas. He was thinking about drawing and painting and modelling and music and collage and writing and acting and dancing and singing and so on. The more ways in which a child can choose to explore something, the more links or connections the child will be able to make and the greater the understanding will be. So, it involves children experimenting, trying things out, developing their skills, their confidence and their competence.

More examples for you to think about:

After a visit to see the marble lions in a square in the town of Modena, children came back and were able to make lions out of clay or out of boxes and junk materials; to dress up as lions; to act like lions; to move like lions; to make up stories about lions, and so on.

Twenty-eight-month-old Polly makes marks on paper and declares, 'It me!'

Twenty-two-month-old Torulf takes a wooden spoon and bashes happily on upturned plastic pots, a saucepan and a metal tin. 'Music!' he announces. When given a drum he tried bashing it with the wooden spoon, with his hands and then with the metal tin.

Representing

'Representing' refers to many of the things already discussed and relates, of course, to exploring, experimenting and playing. The significant thing about this is the child discovering how one thing can stand for or represent another. This is hugely important in coming to understand the world, in which so many things are symbolic. Language itself is symbolic. The words we speak and the words we read and write stand for things and ideas. So, the word 'cat', said or read or written, can be understood by any speaker of English. Numbers are symbols, too. Children, once they have learned about the symbolic function, begin to invent and use their own symbols and marks, and this is the beginnings of an understanding of letters and numbers and literacy itself. Part of this involves children in learning that others may use marks differently – an appreciation that there are different ways of writing words in different languages, for example.

Think about the following examples:

Omar puts the cup on his head, then takes it off and pretends to drink out of it. Then he takes it to the sand tray and fills it with sand. Then he turns it over and hits it with a spoon. Pleased with the sound, he takes another cup – a larger one – and hits that with a spoon too.

An early piece of writing of her name by Chloe at the age of two and commented on by her mother (Figure 3.1):

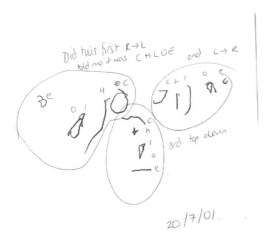

Figure 3.1 Chloe's writing and her mother's comments.

A Healthy Child

'A healthy child' is an interesting and very relevant Aspect, referring to health in terms which include being adequately cared for and fed and being free from illness, but also being emotionally cared for. So, being safe and keeping safe and knowing how to make healthy choices are key factors in the learning and development of young children.

Emotional well-being

'Emotional well-being' refers to emotional stability and resilience, and involves the child in feeling special to someone, being able to express feelings and developing, first, healthy dependence and then healthy independence.

Think about these examples:

'With his father close by the child will confidently explore a new environment, but he will always keep within a radius of about a hundred feet as if joined to his father by an invisible thread and, as if connected by a thread, he will constantly return to his father for reassurance before setting off again.' (Karmiloff-Smith 1994, p. 205)

Danielle (seventeen months): 'The biggest tantrum this week was when she wanted a pushchair that a three-year-old was pushing. She pushed her over even though she was bigger than Danielle and grabbed the pram, and Danielle pushed it to the other end of the room.' (Ibid., p. 221)

Growing and developing

The 'growing and developing' component refers to the recognised importance of things like the child being well nourished, active, rested and protected. It also refers to the child gaining control of the body and acquiring physical skills.

Think about this:

In the day nurseries for the youngest children, called *asili nidi* in Reggio Emilia, everything that takes place is regarded as significant for the learning and development of the children. All the adults working there – including those who cook and clean – are referred to as *pedagogista* (or educationalist) and all activities are bathed in language. The tables on which the babies have their nappies changed have mirrored ceilings above them so that the children can see their images from different angles. There are also mirrors at low levels and set in the floor tiles. When the infants become mobile they can see their images as they crawl on the floor or, when they begin to stand, holding on to objects. In the earliest years, routines of the day predominate and these include being fed, being changed and sleeping. As the babies get older, the times taken up by these routines reduce and are replaced by the increasingly independent children being able to choose freely from what is available.

Keeping safe

In order to keep safe, the young child has to discover boundaries and limits, to learn about the rules (social and other), to know how and when to ask for help, and to learn that it is important to know when to say no and also to anticipate when others will say no.

Think about these examples, some of which are taken from Dunn (1988).

An eighteen-month-old child heads for an electric socket, forbidden twice during the past twenty minutes of observation. Turns to look at observer, smiling. (Dunn 1988, p. 17)

A twenty-four-month-old child, sitting on its mother's knee, kicks her.
MOTHER: Don't kick because that hurts.
CHILD: More hurt (repeats kick).
MOTHER: No!
CHILD: More hurt (repeats kick).

Questioning the application of a rule:

Thirty-six-month-old child cooking with a sibling. Mother in charge.
MOTHER: Would you two like to go and wash your hands? Go and wash your hands, please.
CHILD: Why don't you wash your hands?
MOTHER: Well, it's you two that are doing the cooking.

Healthy choices

The final component, 'healthy choices', refers to helping children learn how to make choices and involves the child in learning about his or her body, beginning to demonstrate her or his own preferences, making decisions and becoming aware of others' and their needs.

Think about these examples and see whether they illustrate for you how children make choices and decisions and show awareness:

Twenty-eight-month-old Lionel says, 'I love this truck. It's the best one in the world. I hate that blue one. It goes too slow. This one is best in the whole wide world.'

Twenty-month-old Keri insists on walking along the balance bar unaided. When first an adult and then an older child try to hold her hand, she hits out, shrieking, 'Me do it!'

As you read through these Aspects and their Components you will realise that there is a considerable degree of overlap between them, and this highlights what is known about how best to support learning and develop: to see it holistically and not in terms of different subjects or learning areas. As the child learns to express preferences, he or she is making choices, making decisions, communicating and sharing meaning. Many aspects of development are involved.

Translating this into practice

Accompanying the Framework is a set of Component cards. Each of these offers practical advice for practitioners in terms of activities and things to offer the children to enhance aspects of learning related to the component, and suggests things to look for when observing the children at play. The cards are useful, but a word of warning: they refer often to stages of development and, as I have suggested earlier in this book, not everyone agrees that there are clear linear stages that apply to all children. The cards also have a section entitled 'Meeting diverse needs' which offers some advice about how to ensure that the needs of children who have English as an additional language, or whose culture and experience are very different from those of the other children and/or the practitioners, or who have experienced stress and trauma in their lives, or who have some specific physical, emotional or learning need, can be met. Spare blank cards are included for practitioners to use for their own planning and there is a CD-ROM and a video which are useful.

NOTE: Birth to Three Matters *is only touched on in this book: the primary focus is still on the Foundation Stage curriculum. Those working with the younger children would be well advised to read the book* Birth to Three Matters: Supporting the Framework of Effective Practice *(Abbott and Langston 2004).*

Summary
- In this chapter we have taken a very brief look at the *Birth to Three Matters* Framework in order to examine recent thinking and practice relating to children, their needs and development before the age of three. The chapter needs to be read with reference to previous and following chapters for a fuller picture to emerge.

Chapter 4

Introduction to the Curriculum guidance to the Foundation Stage

In September 2000 the Qualifications and Curriculum Authority (QCA) produced the Curriculum guidance for the Foundation Stage – a curriculum to apply to children from the age of three to the end of the reception year (that is, the end of the first year of formal schooling). It sets out to prepare the children to meet the demands of the National Curriculum and does this through a series of early learning goals. These were based on an earlier set of what had been called Desirable Outcomes for Children's Learning. The Foundation Stage curriculum pre-dates *Birth to Three Matters* by some years. *Birth to Three Matters* has been discussed first in this book because it makes more sense to look at requirements chronologically and developmentally.

There is an increasing tendency throughout the developed world for planners to believe that the earlier young children start formal learning, the better the results will be. From what you have read in Chapter 1 of this book you will know that the way in which young children learn is different from the way in which older children or adults learn. You will remember the work of Lilian Katz and David Elkind and their findings that children introduced to formal learning at too young an age may actually suffer long-term damage to their desire to be independent, to solve problems, to think for themselves and to carry on being curious.

Experts involved in the development of the new curriculum pleaded with government and planners to bear this in mind. As long ago as 1992, members of the Early Years Curriculum Group published a pamphlet entitled *First Things First: Educating Your Children*. The pamphlet was written as a guide for parents and governors and offered a set of principles which they believed were fundamental to good early years practice. The Foundation Stage, once published, also offered principles.

The principles of *First Things First*

- Early childhood is the foundation on which children build the rest of their lives. It is important and valid in itself and should not be seen as the preparation for the next stage of life or of learning.
- Children develop emotionally, socially, intellectually, morally, physically, spiritually and linguistically and they develop at different rates. All aspects of development are equally important and always interwoven.
- Young children learn from everything that happens to them and do not separate their learning into subjects.
- Young children learn by doing rather than by being told.
- Children learn most effectively when they are actively involved and interested in what they are doing.
- Children need time and space to produce work of quality and depth.
- What children can do rather than what they cannot yet do should be the starting point for their learning.
- Playing and talking are the main ways in which young children learn.

Many regard these as a fine set of principles, based on a recognition of how young children learn best. You may want to compare and contrast these principles with those that follow.

The principles of the Foundation Stage

- Effective education requires both a relevant curriculum and practitioners who understand and are able to implement the curriculum requirements.
- Effective education requires practitioners who understand that children develop rapidly during the early years – physically, intellectually, emotionally and socially.

To ensure that its provision embraces these principles, Amandla Primary School examined its existing practice and made some changes, the first of which was to set up an Early Years Unit made up of the reception classes and the nursery. The headteacher scrutinised the qualifications of the staff and appointed two teachers to the unit: to the reception class, an early years specialist who had been in the nursery, and to the nursery, a newly qualified teacher with two young children of her own. She then placed a nursery nurse in the nursery class and a teaching assistant, who was following a programme for higher-level teaching assistants, in the reception class. The headteacher invited the early years specialist to run a series of after-school meetings for all teachers in the school to look at learning through play, learning through talk, learning through books, learning through first-hand experience and exploration, and learning across the curriculum, indoors and out. She told the staff that the principles of good early years learning were applicable to all children in the primary school. (You will not be surprised to read that she trained as an early years teacher.)

- Practitioners should ensure that all children feel included, secure and valued.
- Parents and practitioners should work together in an atmosphere of mutual respect within which children can have security and confidence.
- No child should be excluded or disadvantaged because of ethnicity, culture or religion, home language, family background, special educational needs, disability, gender or ability.

To ensure that its practice addressed these principles, Amandla formed links with a number of local playgroups, parent organisations and other external agencies. Its staff visited Dumisane Children's Centre, which caters for a very mixed community: more than seventy languages are spoken by the children and their families. Dumisane has a highly regarded parent involvement policy and has worked hard to take account of the views of parents and to hear their voices. One concern has been the parents' unwillingness to accept that children really do learn when they are playing. To deal with this, the school invited in someone from the local university who is an expert in both play and working with parents, including those from different cultures, and this person ran a series of workshops for parents, which were regarded as successful. Amandla went further, however, and invited two of the parents who are themselves teachers to come in and share their experiences of educating and nurturing children in developing countries, and to present their ideas about ways of speaking to and educating young children. Partnership, here, is a real two-way process and an equal relationship.

- Early years experience should build on what children already know and can do.
- To be effective, an early years curriculum should be carefully structured to include three strands:

  - provision for different starting points;
  - relevant and appropriate content to match the different levels of needs;
  - planned and purposeful activity for teaching and learning, indoors and out.

- There should be opportunities for children to engage in activities planned by adults and also those they plan or initiate themselves.
- Practitioners must be able to observe and respond appropriately to children, informed by knowledge of how children develop and learn and a clear understanding of possible next steps in their development and learning.
- Well-planned, purposeful activity and appropriate intervention by practitioners will engage children in the learning process and help them make progress in their learning.

- The learning environment should be well planned and well organised to allow children to have rich and stimulating experience.

Planning is something that many early years practitioners do well because they are used to taking notice of what young children say and do, and then using this as the basis for planning. At both Amandla and Dumisane the early years teams meet every day when the children leave, for a brief and very focused review of what staff have noted during their observations. Suggestions are then made about what might be offered next and more detailed plans are made, including who will be doing what and where and which activities will be offered indoors and out. Staff develop activities to meet the interests of the children, to offer a challenge, and ensure a balance between offering many choices for play as well as some adult-directed activities. At the end-of-the-day-meetings staff also plan which children to observe in detail on the following day.

- Above all, effective learning and development for young children requires high-quality care and education by practitioners.

At a nursery school in Barnet, north London, the headteacher is concerned that all her staff should have appropriate, up-to-date and relevant training. She ensures that all have access to the training on offer in the borough, plans a series of staff development sessions, ensures all staff have opportunities to visit other settings and has encouraged primary helpers to follow courses leading to higher-level teaching assistant qualifications. Here is her rationale for doing this.

> I want all the staff to understand what is known about how young children learn and thrive. I don't want to see any child in the early years groups filling in work sheets or being taught synthetic phonics or having to sit through long whole-school assemblies. I don't want to see the children having to eat in the main dining room or do PE, but I do want to see them having many opportunities inside and out to learn and develop, to play and to be inventive and creative. I want our children to leave the nursery as competent, thinking, expressive, caring and independent learners.

Perhaps you feel that there have been some losses from the earlier work but also some gains. The greatest loss seems to be the *comparative lack of focus on what is known about how young children learn best*. The earlier work talks about the need for children to have both time and space to get deeply involved in what they are doing; to be able to learn by doing rather than by being told; to learn through having their own interests fostered.

Think about four-year old Sacha and the differences between what he does at home and at school. Consider why this might be.

Each morning Sacha is required to find his name card and to trace his name. When he has done that he is directed to the first activity of the day. The teacher reports that Sacha struggles to trace his name, which surprises his mother, who has seen Sacha write his name and the names of his family and friends in the writing he chooses to do at home. When she tells the teacher this, the information is received with a knowing smile, which leads Sacha's mother to feel that she is being perceived as being 'pushy'. She resolves to say no more about what she believes that Sacha can do.

The earlier set of principles also *makes more direct reference to the importance of talk in learning.*

The Foundation Stage curriculum does pay more explicit attention to considering *how to meet the needs of all children and indicates that a balance between adult-directed and child-initiated activities should be found.* Perhaps you noticed that neither set of principles says anything much about the importance of relationships, and when you think back to *Birth to Three Matters*, that seems a glaring omission.

The curriculum guidance to the Foundation Stage lays out clearly a curriculum for children aged three to six in all settings. Despite all you have read about the importance of early learning being holistic and about childhood being a phase in its own right and not the preparation for what is to come, anyone reading the document finds in it six learning areas which look very much like 'subjects', and much indication that children are being prepared for Key Stage 1 of the National Curriculum. Embedded in a description of each learning area is a set of early learning goals, and these are the things the majority of children are expected to know and be able to do at the end of the reception year.

The six *learning areas* are:

- personal, social and emotional development;
- communication, language and literacy;
- mathematical development;
- knowledge and understanding of the world;
- physical development;
- creative development.

The *early learning goals* are the expectations for what most children will reach at the end of the foundation stage. They do not, in themselves, constitute a curriculum. They are organised into the learning areas and provide the basis for planning in order to lay the foundations for future learning. By the end of the Foundation Stage some children will have exceeded the goals, while some will still be working towards them.

The *stepping stones* are described as the steps of progress children make towards the early learning goals and have been designed to help the practitioner identify the knowledge, skills and attitudes that children need to be helped to develop in order to reach the goals. They are not age related and progress will vary from child to child, from learning area to learning area. They are presented in hierarchical order, but it is important to note that the guidance does state that not all children will learn in the linear fashion that such a hierarchical ordering suggests.

Think about how one playgroup – the Rainbow Playgroup – set out the principles that will underpin its curriculum and identified the goals it will follow.

We are going to *set up activities, indoors and out*, which will allow children the following experiences:

(a)   opportunities to develop motor skills;
(b)   opportunities to use tools;
(c)   opportunities to make plans;
(d)   opportunities for speaking and listening;
(e)   opportunities for reading and writing;
(f)   opportunities for counting, for sorting, for matching, for one-to-one correspondence;
(g)   opportunities for exploring space and shape;
(h)   opportunities to explore pattern;
(i)   opportunities to express ideas through drawing, painting, using clay and malleable materials, through music, through dance, through imaginative play;
(j)   opportunities to understand the physical world through observing, making guesses, trying things out;
(k)   opportunities to understand the world through going on visits, looking at images and artefacts, through books and stories, through reflecting the languages and cultures of our community;
(l)   opportunities to develop social skills through role play, the routines of the day, through sharing and negotiating.

We will make sure that the *activities we provide make human sense* to the children so that they can see the purpose of the activities and build on their previous experience.

We will *observe children regularly*, keep notes on what we see and then share these with one another in an attempt to understand what each child is doing, where each child is. We will plan activities based on these assessments.

We will make our notes *available to parents* and invite them to tell us about the child at home. This will take some time to develop, but it is one of our goals for the coming year.

One member of staff is taking *responsibility for special needs*, so if we are worried about a child she will be our first port of call.

We are going to meet once a week after hours in order to *improve our own skills*. We have decided that our focus for this year will be on how we can support the children's learning through intervention. We are going to invite in some guest speakers to talk to us and have already started looking for books or videos to support us in doing this.

You can see from this plan just how many of the principles of high-quality early years education this group have taken on. They have planned a programme for themselves and for the children which is aimed at taking learning forward. In subsequent chapters we will return to this group and see how their plans are taking shape.

A European perspective

In the wealthy area of Reggio Emilia in northern Italy the provision of high-quality childcare and education has been a priority of all the local people since the end of the Second World War. Led by an idealist and educationalist, Loris Malaguzzi (who has already been mentioned in this book), local people obtained the resources and the support to establish a number of nurseries which are still the envy of the developed world – so much so that the number of visitors to these nurseries has had to be limited in recent years.

There are a number of features that make the provision special. First, parents and other people in the local community are involved in the management of these nurseries and their words are listened to. Second, everything that happens is documented. Careful records are kept of every aspect of the work and these are analysed in order that successful things can be replicated and unsuccessful things dropped. All the nurseries are in purpose-built facilities and the architects and planners have to take account of the social, emotional, health, physical, creative and educational needs of the children and workers when designing the building and the equipment to go in it. Staff have good working conditions and an ongoing programme of in-service training.

Most impressive, however, is the quality of the work of the children. Visitors are often stunned by the intensity of the children's concentration as they draw and paint, use the computers, design and construct, make and send messages to one another and explore the physical space. The philosophy of the nurseries is that childhood is important in its own right and that children should encounter a range of meaningful experiences and activities in order that they become able to represent and re-represent what they have seen and heard and learned.

Think about this example taken from a nursery school in Modena and consider what makes the experiences meaningful for these particular children:

In a nursery in Modena a project developed around the theme of lions. In Modena the cathedral, set in a magnificent square, has stone lions outside it. All the families of Modena use the square as a meeting place and all the children regard the lions as familiar. The staff took a group of children to visit the lions. The children took with them clipboards and pencils and they were invited to draw the lions if they wanted to. Back at the nursery a host of other activities were on offer. Some children drew the lions in pencil and then made large and brilliantly coloured paintings. Some made giant lions out of large cardboard boxes and junk materials. Some dressed up as lions and made up stories or dances. Some made lions out of clay, using tools skilfully and appropriately.

You can see from this example the ways in which the children were able to represent their ideas and feelings about the lions in a range of ways. Remember how learning involves the establishment of connections between brain cells. In this example, each time a representation was made (a drawing or a model or a dance or a poem), another set of connections was established. More than that, each time a new representation was made, something new was discovered or thought or felt by the child.

Now think about the next example and consider what you might have done to take the learning of the children forward:

In a different nursery in the same region the teachers (all workers are given the title of teacher) were concerned that children's links with the nursery might be damaged over the long summer holiday, so they gave each child a box and invited the children to put in the box anything they chose to remind them of the summer. The children were asked to bring the filled boxes back to the nursery when term resumed. One little girl had in her box a bus ticket. Through discussion the staff discovered that it was the ticket she had used to go and visit her grandparents, who lived at the seaside. When she was asked what she had seen at the seaside she surprised the adults by saying she had seen 'arms and legs'. They had been expecting her to say 'buckets and spades' or 'ice creams'. As sensitive and exploring teachers, the adults explored further and discovered that the seaside town the little girl had visited was situated on a steep hillside, and in order to get to the beach she had to walk down steep streets. Put yourself in the position of a four-year-old and you will realise that in doing this you are indeed surrounded by a forest of arms and legs. The staff started talking to the children about what was meant by the word 'crowd' and they discovered that most of the children thought that a crowd meant a group of people all going in the same direction.

What would you have done? Here is what the staff at the nursery above did. They first took the children out into the square so that they could be part of a crowd and notice that not all the people were going in the same direction. They then suggested that the children draw one another – from the front, from the back and in profile. Using the photocopier, they then enlarged some of the drawings and shrank others. The final versions were coloured in by the children, cut out and mounted on card so that they would stand upright. The resulting collection of images was placed upright in a large box so that the children had a symbolic representation of a crowd.

The work of these Italian nursery schools is underpinned by a clear philosophy which embraces many of the points outlined in the principles for high-quality early learning. The type of curriculum that emerges from this is one that can be described as developmental. Such a curriculum takes as its starting point a *dynamic view of development*. This recognises that human development changes over time and with experience so that the ways in which young children learn are recognised as different from the ways in which older children and adults learn. Such a dynamic view also recognises the impact of what is called 'delayed impact', which refers to the ways in which early experience may affect later functioning, particularly with regard to the development of self-esteem, social development, feelings and dispositions. The third aspect of a developmental viewpoint is the long-term cumulative effect of frequent experiences. This implies that something that happens to a young child once or twice may be beneficial in the short term, but repeated exposure over a long period of time may have damaging effects.

These are quite difficult ideas to grasp but they are important to those of us concerned with promoting early learning and development. Malaguzzi (personal communication, 1992) said that he knew that once children started school they would be exposed to what he described as tedious and meaningless tasks – things like colouring in, joining the dots, tracing their names, and completing jigsaw puzzles. He urged us:

> Look around you at the remarkable creative and original things the children can do and then think about how the school teachers, by ignoring all that children have already done and achieved by the time they start school, make the children feel stupid and ignorant and give them things that offer no intellectual challenge. The teachers in schools keep telling us that we don't 'teach' the children properly. By that they mean that we don't train them to do meaningless things. I say to them, 'We give our children a sense of their own identity, opportunities to express their

thoughts and ideas through some of the hundred languages at their disposal (writing, drawing, building, designing, acting, dancing, singing) and we believe that we lay a foundation which will allow the children to get through their schooling with their attitude to learning and discovery undamaged. That is our job.' I say to them, 'Maybe you should learn from us and not expect us to prepare the children for years of tedium and boredom.'

(Personal communication, 1992)

Contrast this developmental approach with an example offered by Lilian Katz. In an American pre-school a group of four-year-olds were engaged in what Katz describes as the 'calendar ritual'. Katz describes what happened as follows:

> With the children seated on the floor facing a large calendar showing the month of February, the teacher asks them what day it is today. They call out the days of the week in what appears to be random fashion, and by chance none offers the correct answer; which is Thursday. The teacher then asks, 'What day was it yesterday?' The same array of guesses is offered, which fortunately includes Wednesday. She responds, 'That's right! So what day is it today?' Eventually she coaxes them into agreeing on the correct answer. When she asks next for the date (the 19th) no one replies. She then asks one of the children to come forward and write the correct numbers in the appropriate empty box on the calendar. When he hesitates, she suggests that he look at the number for yesterday. Unfortunately, he looks in the box above rather than to the left of the empty one. Because it contains the number 12, the child says 13. Pointing out that he has looked 'the wrong way' the teacher asks, 'What comes after 18?' She thereby persuades him to agree on the date, which he manages to write almost legibly in the box.'

(Personal communication, 1988)

Katz points out that the children involved were far too young to understand the concept of the date, but because they are eager to please the teacher they behave with great courtesy, attempting to produce the answer that will satisfy her. Katz goes on to say that if something like this happened to young children once or twice in the early years it would probably have no deleterious effect. But in many pre-school settings in the United States and in many reception classes in schools, this type of decontextualised activity happens with monotonous regularity, day in, day out. As I have said before, young children will learn from all experiences and they may learn undesirable as well as desirable things. For Katz, then, the developmental question is not so much what children can do or even how they learn. The question is what should they do that will best help their learning and development in the long term. Katz urges that those working with young children not only pay attention to what is known about how young children learn, but also take heed of the long-term cumulative effects of the experiences they encounter. For us, then, the message is that the curriculum is not only about what children should learn, but, crucially, how they should learn. What we, the adults, do is crucial to their learning and development in the long term.

One way or many?

Most of the research and theory quoted here and, indeed, in most of the books on child development you will encounter comes from a Western perspective. It is important to remember that the users of our pre-school services come from a range of backgrounds, with varying expectations and differing values. In their book *Preschool in Three Cultures*, Tobin *et al*. examine an American pre-school, a Japanese pre-school and a Chinese pre-school, and their findings provide much food for thought.

In American pre-schools the pursuit of happiness is often one of the explicit goals, whereas Chinese pre-schools are regarded as places of serious learning where if the children are happy as they learn, so much the better, but happiness is a by-product and not a goal. The Japanese pre-schools aim to produce children who are childlike, and this means that they will often be happy but may also be angry, frustrated, lonely or selfish. The outcome of this is that Japanese children are encouraged to learn through play in a loosely planned environment where the adults stay on the fringes of children's play and do not intervene in order to support and extend learning.

It is obvious, too, that pre-schools in affluent societies will be better resourced and equipped than those in poorer countries. American pre-schools provide children with an overwhelming amount of toys, books, miniature versions of adult things (like irons and Hoovers), outdoor equipment, and so on. On the walls are children's drawings and images of 'happy' things – like cartoon characters, animals dressed like people and nursery rhymes. The question arises as to whether such an abundance of equipment is necessary for learning and development. If the answer to this question is yes, ill-equipped playgroups will feel that they have no chance to compete with their better-equipped counterparts. A Japanese pre-school teacher commented as follows:

> We don't have a make-believe corner, but children in our school play lots of imaginary games. They play house and store and fireman. You don't need costumes and plastic dishes to play house. You don't need a fireman's hat to pretend you're a fireman. I don't think that children need all of those special things to play. Don't teachers in America believe children have imagination?
>
> (Tobin *et al*. 1989, p. 155)

This may be consoling for you if you are struggling to gather together all the materials and resources you see so glossily displayed in educational catalogues. It is worth bearing in mind that more than half the world's children learn and play using natural, found and real materials.

The importance of play as a mode of learning

Although many parents recognise that children play, and through their play learn, many also believe that once children start in the nursery or school they should put playing away and start to 'learn for real'. The issue of play as a mode or way of learning is something anyone involved with the learning of young children needs to read about, think about and come to understand. What needs to be understood is what is meant by the word 'play' and what makes it an effective way of learning for all of us. What else needs to be understood is that although play is highly regarded as a way of learning in the Western world, it is not a universal or the sole way in which young children can learn. Young children will learn through interactions with other children and with adults. They will learn by doing things. They will learn by looking and listening and, later, by reading and by symbolising.

In 1996 the Curriculum and Assessment Authority for Wales published a consultation document on its proposal to introduce its 'Desirable Outcomes for Children's Learning before Compulsory School Age'. The document talks in some detail about the early years curriculum, reminding readers that it is about the child and that it is concerned not only with content but also with the *context* of learning. In other words, *the process* is just as important as the product or outcome. The Welsh document goes on to talk in some detail about the importance of play.

Think about what the Welsh document says about play (summarised below). How does it advance your understanding?

Children's play is a very serious business indeed. It needs concentrated attention. It is all about perseverance, attending to detail, learning and concentrating – characteristics usually associated with work. Play is work and work is play for the young child. Play is not only crucial to the way children become self-aware and the way in which they learn the rules of social behaviour, it is also fundamental to intellectual development. Young children learn most effectively when they are actively involved in first hand experiences. Young children's learning is a hands-on business. An education service for young children is about the child. It is about adults understanding, inspiring and challenging the child's talent to learn. Adults' involvement in children's play is of vital importance. Good early years educators are there to help children, to guide their play, to offer choices when the playing flags, to challenge children with care and sensitivity, to encourage them and to move their learning along.

This is a thoughtful account and one worth reading again and again and taking very seriously. It helps any practitioner become able to explain to many cynical parents and colleagues just what it is about play that makes it a prime mode of learning for children. The document goes on to look at what it calls 'the principle of appropriateness'. This really illustrates the developmental approach described earlier. Young children vary in rates of growth and development. You will have come across four-year-olds who look like six-year-olds and four-year-olds who look like two-year-olds. The same variation is true of intellectual development. A curriculum designed for young children must acknowledge this fact and those working with young children need to understand that we cannot say that all four-year-olds should be able to write their names, for example. What we can say is that most four-year-olds given the opportunity will be able to write their names, recognising that there will be some children who will not learn to write their names until they are five or six. This does not necessarily indicate that these children are 'slow learners'; rather, it suggests that these children have not yet developed an interest in learning to write their names. Their concerns and interests lie elsewhere. This again is an important point and one worth remembering when you are presented with development stages or sets of so-called milestones.

Summary

- An early years curriculum is about more than content: it is about the context in which learning takes place. This means that the process is just as important as the outcomes.
- An early years curriculum is about the child. Childhood should be regarded as important in its own right and not seen as preparation for the next stage or phase.
- The views of parents and users are important and should be considered when developing the curriculum.
- Workers need to understand the importance of play for learning and be able to explain this clearly to parents. They need, too, to be respectful of and attentive to the views of parents who may have had different experiences.
- Resources should be there to support learning. Learning is possible even when resources are limited.
- Young children vary enormously in their rates of development and this should be recognised and acknowledged by workers.

continued on next page

- Workers need to remember that young children learn best by doing rather than by being told, and that language is essential for learning.
- Children need time and space in order to pursue their concerns in depth. The day should not be broken down into small segments of time and the routines of the day should be seen as opportunities to extend learning.

Chapter 5

Living and communicating in a social world

In this chapter we examine in detail what children are expected to know and do by the time they reach compulsory school age in two learning areas: personal, social and emotional development, and communication, language and literacy. More importantly, we look at ways of offering activities and resources to help children attain the early learning goals at the end of the Foundation Stage in ways which fit in with what is known about how young children learn best.

You will recognise that the learning area of personal, social and emotional development is critical for young children and that their personal, social and emotional well-being impacts on every aspect of their lives and of their learning and development. It is clear how closely this learning area relates to some of the Aspects of the *Birth to Three Matters* Framework. A strong child, a healthy child, a child who can communicate with others is likely to also be a competent learner.

The Curriculum Framework suggests that practitioners should pay particular attention to the following:

> **Establishing and maintaining constructive relations with children, with other practitioners, between practitioners and children, with parents and with workers from other agencies and in doing this to take account of differences and of different needs and expectations.**

Rainbow Playgroup builds into its routines that staff meet for a brief time every afternoon in order to review the day and to plan for the next day. The staff believe that in doing this they are building relationships with one another and learning from one another about all the children. We will see in sections to come what they do to build positive relationships with and between children and with parents and those from other agencies.

> **Finding opportunities to give positive encouragement to children, with practitioners acting as positive role models.**

At Thomas à Kempis Nursery the staff have worked very hard to ensure that they have at least one male member of staff because they feel it is very important for all the children to have a male role model. They also have a policy of appointing people from the local community speaking the local languages in order to give positive encouragement to all children.

Planning opportunities for children to work alone and in small and large groups.

The headteacher of Mahatma Gandhi Primary School is very aware of the fact that she has not had specialised training as an early years educator. She always consults the head of early years when making or changing policy. Together they decided that for the youngest children large-group activities – like story time – can be daunting and now ensure that there are at least two different groups at story time and children can either choose or be allocated to the one deemed the most relevant and suitable. The head of early years talks to staff about offering opportunities throughout each day for children to work and play in small groups, to come together in larger groups and to be allowed to play alone if they choose to.

Ensuring that there is time and space for children to focus on activities and experiences and develop their own interests.

The focus here is on play – which has been defined as a mode of learning in which children follow their own interests and are in control of their own agenda. At Mahatma Gandhi Primary School the early years coordinator has developed an observation format for staff to use in their regular written observations of children, and one of the things staff are asked to do is note how long the child spent on the activity being observed. This is one way of making time and space a crucial element of the curriculum.

Planning activities to promote learning across all aspects of development – emotional, moral, spiritual, social and intellectual.

One of the key themes of early childhood education is that learning in the early years is holistic – which means that it does not take place in separate subject areas. So, a child exploring an interest or involved in an activity will be developing language, aspects of mathematics, perhaps; almost certainly something to do with knowledge and understanding of the world; some physical skills or learning, and so on. Educators may plan for separate learning areas but need to realise that what the children learn will not be limited to that learning area.

Planning experiences to help children develop autonomy and the disposition to learn and planning for the development of independence skills, particularly for children who are highly dependent upon adult support for personal care.

Back at Rainbow Playgroup, staff are focusing at the moment on ways of promoting independence and thinking particularly about the youngest children, those requiring adult help, those lacking self-esteem and those who might be described as vulnerable. One of the things they are considering is pairing these children with more confident and experienced children. Another thing they are talking about is how they will work alongside children, helping them take steps in their learning that they support (through modelling, physical help, talk) and then removing the support, allowing the child to achieve independently. You will recognise this as scaffolding learning.

Personal, social and emotional development

Judy Dunn says:

> Children are born into a complex social world: from infancy on, they are active participants in a world of other people – adults and children, familiar and not so familiar others. On common-sense grounds it seems reasonable to argue that it is important for them to begin to understand the intentions, feelings and actions of others who share their world and to comprehend the social rules of that world.
>
> (1988, p. 1)

She goes on to illustrate how this takes place. Human infants are predisposed to learn about the characteristics of people. They are very attentive to shapes and patterns that are like human faces and respond to sounds similar to that of the human female voice. At the age of only two months they can differentiate between someone who wants to communicate with them and someone talking to someone else. By the age of seven or eight months, babies seem really attuned to different emotional expressions in adults, and they begin to play cooperative games like peekaboo. They share in the daily routines of feeding, changing and dressing, and soon begin to demonstrate that they share a communicative framework with others – waving goodbye, eye-pointing to what they want, smiling with pleasure. They are highly social and sociable beings.

Colwyn Trevarthen (1998) goes further and looks at how children come to learn about the culture into which they have been born. He asks why it is that very young children are so keen to learn the language and all the other habits and customs and rituals and beliefs of the community around them. He says that a three-year-old child is a socially aware person who can make and keep friends, who can negotiate and cooperate with many different people in many different situations. For Trevarthen, young children primarily make sense by sharing. They use their emotions and the emotions of others to categorise experiences that will help them cooperate.

The early learning goals for personal, social and emotional development

Set 1: Early learning goals for dispositions and attitudes

Continue to be interested in, excited by and motivated to learn.

Be confident to try new activities, initiate ideas and speak in a familiar group.

Maintain attention, concentrate, and sit quietly when appropriate.

We know that the human infant is intensely curious and seeks to understand all aspects of the world into which he or she is born. This curiosity, which is innate, is what Lilian Katz calls a *positive disposition*. You will remember that Katz says such dispositions should be encouraged and fostered, and has demonstrated how they can be damaged through too early exposure to formal learning. Children's curiosity is most likely to be promoted when they are able to follow their own concerns or interests in a stimulating and challenging environment which offers first-hand experience, talk and appropriate adult intervention.

Think about what this example given by Mary Smith suggests:

> The children were interested in some bees in the centre garden. One boy wanted to know how honey was made. He suggested that they make some in the centre. Mary asked him how this could be done and he said that they needed to get together some flowers – daisies, buttercups and dandelions that were growing wild in the garden. He duly gathered these together and put them in a plastic tray. Daniel (aged 4.6) then said 'We have to pick out the pollen from the middle of each flower' and then spent a considerable amount of time doing this. When he was satisfied that he had got all the pollen he asked Mary to get him a cup and spoon. Daniel put the pollen in the cup and stirred it around a bit. After a while Mary asked him what was happening to the pollen. 'Nothing' he replied. 'We have to add apple juice and then we will have honey.'
>
> (Smith, in Smidt (ed.) 1998, pp. 148–9)

Children's curiosity runs the risk of being damaged when they are asked to do inappropriate things – things that do not make 'human sense' to them. Before the advent of the Foundation Stage many children in reception classes were being asked to engage in rote learning, the completion of meaningless tasks and the solving of decontextualised problems. The Foundation Stage offers the possibility for learning in this year to be more rooted in activities that will maintain children's curiosity, excitement and desire to learn. Where this happens, it is likely that children will have the confidence to try new activities, and within a supportive environment they are likely to speak in a familiar group as long as they know that what they say will matter to those listening to them.

Anyone who has paid attention to young children knows that when they are really interested in something they are able to get deeply immersed in it and persevere and concentrate over long periods of time. Providing opportunities for them to do this is a vital principle of quality early years education, and there is much here for those in reception classes to consider. But you might want to think more carefully about expecting children to 'sit quietly'.

Take time to consider carefully some of the issues raised by this learning outcome in light of what you have learned about how it is believed most young children learn best.

- Do you think the day in the reception class should consist of different 'lessons'?
- Do you think children should have 'playtime'?
- Do you think the day should be more like a traditional nursery day – long, unbroken stretches of time in which to get deeply involved and ongoing access to outdoor play?

Here is an example from a reception class where the teacher had brought in some plants plus magnifiers for the children to use. She had wanted them to be able to describe plants using the magnifier to highlight particular features. The children all had English as an additional language, and during the teacher's lengthy explanation they were largely silent. Then one child spotted a snail on a leaf, and the teacher took the opportunity to abandon her plan and be led by the children. The little group, which had been largely passive and silent, suddenly came to life. They touched the snail, looked at it and discussed passionately whether it was dead or asleep when it withdrew into its shell. One child went off to find a program on the computer that had snails in it while another chose some paper and pastels to draw a snail. The activity went on throughout the morning, with the children deeply engrossed in the activities offered.

We do, of course, want children, at some stage, to concentrate and maintain attention, but do we also want them to 'sit quietly when appropriate'? Children will listen to something that interests, amuses or entertains them. You have only to watch children at the theatre or watching a programme on television or listening to a story for evidence of this. We do want children to be able to do this in situations which are significant for them. In such sessions we are happy to have children contribute their own ideas and to discuss and comment to one another and to the adults. We rarely, if ever, have reason to want silence with such young children. It is, after all, more a way of controlling children than a way of enhancing their learning and development. A danger implicit in having sitting quietly as a goal is that teachers and practitioners might be tempted to teach in ways that are not entirely appropriate to young children. Defining what we mean by 'appropriate' in this goal is important, and we need to consider whether we want young children to sit quietly because they want to see and hear or whether we want them to sit quietly as a means of controlling them. One obvious example is in reception classes, where teachers are sometimes under pressure to introduce some of the aspects of the Literacy Hour and do this by getting children to sit in a large group, being passive, for rather too long. We will discuss this in more detail later in this chapter.

Set 2: Early learning goals for self-confidence and self-esteem

> Respond to significant experiences showing a range of feelings when appropriate.

> Have a developing awareness of their own needs, views and feelings and be sensitive to the needs, views and feelings of others.

> Have a developing respect for their own cultures and beliefs and those of other people.

Think about the following examples and consider whether the children's responses seem appropriate to you:

When Hannah was just five years old she saw the film *ET* on television and when ET appeared to have died, she wept.

Abby came to nursery very angry for a week or so. Before that she had seemed very settled, so we asked her carer if anything had changed at home. We were distressed to find that Abby's mother had been admitted to hospital and realised that the child was displaying emotions appropriate to her distress.

Do you think that young children should always be happy or are there times when it is
appropriate for them to be sad or angry or jealous or scared?

Diane McClellan and Lilian Katz (1992) have developed a checklist which
practitioners can use to help them understand how individual children can be
supported as they grow in social skilfulness. Items on the list include the
following:

- The child is usually in a positive mood.
- The child usually copes with rebuffs and reverses adequately.
- The child shows the capacity to empathise.
- The child displays the capacity for humour.
- The child does not seem to be acutely or chronically lonely.

Katz also offers practitioners ways of assessing children's 'range of affect'.
What she means by this is looking to see whether any child displays a
range of emotions: joy, sorrow, anger, relief, etc. She argues that a child
whose emotions are of low intensity may be having some difficulties which
a practitioner should know about. Katz is clear that emotions we might
regard as negative – such as sadness – involve the child in knowing about
other associated emotions which are often positive. We feel sad when we feel
not cared for or when a loved one goes away. In other words, in order to feel
sad we have to know what it is to feel cared for or happy or loved. Perhaps
what you have just read affects your initial responses to the questions raised
above.

Judy Dunn has illustrated how young children move from being egocentric, through an awareness of their own needs, views and feelings to understanding and being sensitive to the views, needs and feelings of others.
A group of practitioners contributed the following examples to illustrate
this. Read their comments and see whether you can find evidence of young
children being sensitive to their own needs, feelings and opinions and to
the views, feelings and needs of others.

When my daughter was three she was given a doll as a birthday present from
her grandmother and she burst into tears and said, 'I really wanted a car.'
She had no sense that she was upsetting her Gran. A year later she was given
a copy of a book she already has. 'I've got this, Gran, but it's OK because
mine is old and scruffy.' In a year she had moved on to knowing that her actions
and words can have an effect on someone else and that she has the power to
hurt someone's feelings. Does this surprise you?

The children in the reception class are very protective of one another when a supply teacher visits. They always tell me when I return who cried and why and what they did to 'make it better'. I make a note of the children who comment and record these comments in their profiles as a record of their developing maturity in terms of personal, social and emotional development. Does this surprise you?

Set 3: Early learning goals for sense of community

> Understand that people have different needs, views, cultures and beliefs and that these need to be treated with respect.

> Understand that they can expect others to treat their needs, views, cultures and beliefs with respect.

All our children are growing up in a rich and multicultural world. This applies to children growing up in rural areas where there are few people of other cultures as much as it does to those in richly diverse inner-city communities. In order for children to develop respect for different cultures, beliefs and languages it is important that they encounter adults who enjoy the diversity of our society and show the languages, cultures and religions of the children equal respect. You may want to consider whether this is best done by celebrating the odd festival and occasionally offering some of the traditional foods to the children or whether it should be more deeply embedded in the everyday activities offered to the children. In other words, should Foundation Stage settings think that it is enough to celebrate Chinese New Year, for example, or do they need to go more deeply into this issue?

Think about how this might affect you in your setting. Do you think it is worthwhile for you to celebrate festivals like Eid or Diwali or Chinese New Year? And if you do that do you think you go far enough in equipping young children to live in a richly diverse world?

Here is how one London teacher, Birgit Voss, describes how she and her co-workers prepare for the coming term:

> I make a note of the different languages our little community will be using for the next four months: Gujarati, Bengali, Turkish, Urdu, Cantonese, Arabic, Farsi, German and, of course, English. I check these against our present resources. We have cassette story and video story tapes in all the languages but Cantonese. We have plenty of writing samples, newspapers and magazines in Chinese as we had some Chinese-speaking children earlier. When we celebrated Chinese New Year – the Year of the Dog – we stocked up during a visit to the local Chinese supermarket. We also have appropriate clothes, fabrics and home-base equipment and lots of pictures.

The parents seemed very open, friendly and cooperative during the home visit. I am sure they would love to make some story tapes, maybe sing some songs for us. Something to organise.

(Voss, in Smidt (ed.) 1998, p. 48)

Voss goes on to explain that the children in her nursery class learn from first-hand experience by building on what they already know and states that this approach is ideally suited to the learning needs of young bilingual children. You can see from the example how the celebration of culture and language is embedded in the everyday activities. The home corner is equipped with arte-facts and printed materials and pictures that reflect this. The books and stories and songs are available in languages additional to English. In an environment like this, children are likely to respond with enthusiasm, interest and respect for the world around them. Voss, who is herself bilingual, understands how powerfully one's language is tied up with one's identity and self-esteem. There is no mention of respect for languages in the early learning goals but it is deeply embedded in the principles and underpinning philosophy of the Foundation Stage.

You may be interested and, perhaps, shocked to learn how soon young children pick up negative attitudes to people from other groups. Using large fabric 'Persona' dolls representing children from different groups, Glenda Mac-Naughton carried out some research with pre-school children in Melbourne, Australia. She found that all the white Australian children were happy to play with the white middle-class-looking dolls and recognised them as being 'Australian'. When it came to a Vietnamese doll, this was totally rejected by the children, and none of them chose to play with the Aboriginal doll, although some reluctantly said it might be Australian. Deeply racist views were apparent in children under the age of six.

Set 4: The early learning goals for making relationships

Form good relationships with adults and peers.

Work as part of a group or class, taking turns and sharing fairly, understanding that there need to be agreed values and codes of behaviour for groups of people, including adults and children, to work together harmoniously.

Children are most likely to form good relationships with adults and peers where they themselves are taken seriously, treated with respect and invited to learn in an environment which has both familiar and new things and experiences. It is interesting that there is no mention of building self-esteem in these early learning goals although, again, it is contained in the underlying principles. Many practitioners believe that this is something they strive to achieve, and something that they need to pay careful attention to is ensuring that there is no clash between the values of home and the values of the setting. Children are most likely to feel good about themselves when they are accepted and valued. Most of what children have learned when they start in any pre-school setting has come from home. Where there is a clash between the values of home and those of the setting, children's confidence and self-esteem is damaged.

This raises an important and difficult question. How are practitioners expected to reconcile their values and their understanding of child development with the views and desires of parents? Eve Gregory graphically describes the experience of the teacher of a Chinese child in Northampton:

> Tony enters school smiling . . .
>   A month later, Tony's behaviour has undergone a complete change. His smile has disappeared, replaced, in Mrs G's words, by a 'dead-pan look' which 'you can't seem to get through to'.
>
> (Gregory and Bianes 1994, pp. 18, 21)

Gregory goes on to explain how, in an effort to regain Tony's initial enthusiasm for school, Mrs G visits the family at home, taking with her an attractive dual-language picture/story book which she invites the family to share with him. Tony's grandfather refuses to accept the book, stating that Tony cannot have the book until he can read the words in it. Tony's grandfather goes on to show disgust at Tony's attempts to write his name in English – ToNy. He states, 'This is from his English school. This is rubbish. . . . Look. He can't even write his name yet!' The teacher, Mrs G, has a clearly thought-out philosophy about how young children learn and describes this philosophy as being 'child-centred'.

The important point, Gregory believes, is that discontinuity between home and school or setting is more damaging to children's confidence and self-esteem – and hence to their learning and development – than the adoption of an accepted model of teaching.

What do you learn from this?

Practitioners need to listen to parents to treat their views and experience with respect and to make sure that they are able to explain clearly why they are doing things so that family members can understand. Discontinuity between home and school does not only apply to children who have languages other than English. In her book *Ways with Words*, Shirley Brice Heath (1983) showed how, in one community in the United States, some children came to school with values which matched those of the school while others did not. All the children were competent learners, fluent speakers of their own languages, and well aware of the social rules and mores of their communities. Yet once in school those whose experience was different from that of the teachers and whose cultures were unfamiliar began to fail.

> Work as part of a group or class, taking turns and sharing fairly, understanding that there need to be agreed values and codes of behaviour for groups of people, including adults and children, to work harmoniously together to establish effective relationships with other children and with adults.

Children in well-run Foundation Stage settings will have opportunities to play alone, in pairs, in small groups and sometimes to come together for large-group activities. As they do this they learn to work alongside others, sometimes sharing and taking turns. Where adults talk to them and model appropriate behaviour, they come to work out and internalise the social rules governing what is appropriate in their setting. With support, they move from playing on their own to playing alongside other children. As they get older, they begin to interact in their play and, by the time they have reached the age of four, many of them will be engaged in what is known as 'cooperative play'. In such play, children collaborate on a shared project or topic. In your setting you will want to ensure that there are opportunities for such play. But do remember that children may continue to need to engage in solitary or parallel play beyond the Foundation Stage.

In some settings children have to learn that one of the rules is 'no guns'; children are not allowed to bring guns to school or to make them out of Lego or anything else. The idea is to try to deal with aggression and to encourage behaviour that is regarded as positive. Penny Holland (2003) has written an interesting book looking at the reality of what happens in places where there is zero tolerance to guns and rough play. What happens is that this behaviour (mainly relating to boys) goes 'underground'. Boys remain aggressive and their aggression emerges in different forms. Holland is interested in allowing boys to talk about their feelings – their anger or jealousy or sense of inadequacy – and to allow gun play in an environment where things are openly discussed. This is similar to some of the work done by Vivian Gussin Paley, who uses story-making in the classroom as a way of dealing with feelings which are sometimes regarded as negative.

Set 5: The early learning goals for behaviour and self-control

> Understand what is right, what is wrong and why.

> Consider the consequences of their words and actions for themselves and others.

In settings where children have opportunities to discuss classroom events and those that occur in their lives away from the setting they begin to refine their concepts of right and wrong.

Think about what this example from the reception class at Amandla School says about how the teacher was able to help Charley consider right and wrong.

ALEX: Miss, Charley hit me.

TEACHER: Is that true, Charley? Did you hit Alex? (No reply.)

TEACHER: I hope you can remember that story we read yesterday, children, about the new child who was bullied at school and went home crying. Do you remember, Charley? (No answer.)

TAKLIMA: I remember that story. It was sad. I don't want anybody to hit me or bully me. I like school.

TEACHER: I am really pleased you remember the story so well, Taklima. Nobody likes to be hurt or to get bullied. I think Charley must have been really angry about something and forgotten about one of our rules about hitting. Is that right, Charley? (Child nods.)

TEACHER: Do you want to say anything to me or to Alex or to any of the children?

CHARLEY: Alex broke my model and I was cross. I won't hit him again, but he mustn't break my things any more.

Through discussion in a non-punitive environment, Charley had the chance to consider the impact both of Alex's behaviour on her and of her actions on him.

Set 6: Early learning goals relating to self-care

Dress and undress independently and manage their own personal hygiene.

Seek and use activities and resources independently.

These are two very different but clearly related goals. The first refers to helping children to learn to care for their own physical needs. This builds on what children are doing at home and have been doing in playgroups or crèches or day care centres. The second is one that relates directly to helping children have the confidence to take charge, to some extent, of their own activities and their own learning.

Think about these two contrasting settings and decide which is more likely to foster this goal.

The Free Play Playgroup runs for three mornings a week in a church hall in a small village in Essex. The children have great difficulty in having free choice because of the lack of storage space. Staff put out a selection of toys and activities, and children do have some limited choice about what they want to do. Although the staff have been advised to spend some money on large containers which can be placed on the floor, labelled clearly and made available to the children, they will not do this and think that the children will 'just make a mess'. The children are taken outdoors to play for half an hour during each session.

At the Sunshine Playgroup, which is also on offer for three mornings a week in a local hall, the ethos is very different. Staff have bought a large selection of containers in which they have put small world toys, construction toys and dressing-up clothes, and these are always available to the children. In addition there is always a book area, a graphics area, paints and models and junk available for making things, musical instruments, and water and sand trays. The doors to the outside are always open and there are sand and water trays outdoors, a well-equipped woodwork bench, large milk creates, wheeled toys, prams, and so on.

Children who find themselves in a well-structured and well-planned learning environment will know that they can follow their own interests and find the things they need for themselves. A well-set-out environment has a place for everything – a place that is accessible and evident to children. There are labels in the form of pictures and words. Time is spent on helping the children know what can be found where, and children are expected, as part of their learning, to clear away at the end of each session. Good practitioners induct children into the rules of the setting and in doing this help children understand why rules are needed.

Think about what Ms Singh does in her reception class:

At the beginning of the year I always talk to the children about where things belong, how to put them away and why it is important to care for them. We often talk about what would happen if they leave the lids off the pens, or fold the pages of books. The children come up with rules for themselves. I don't have rules saying things like 'only four children in the sand' because it seems to me that the children can be self-regulating and will appreciate that when activities are overcrowded play is damaged. I depend on the children to sort things out for themselves, and mostly they do. I find that when I don't have to be busy making sure they are keeping to imposed rules I have more time to really interact with them or observe them.

In an environment like this, the development of children's independence is fostered, and children learn quickly that they have the capacity to make choices, find what they need and sometimes to change their plans. Children are expected to learn through play, and the adults become not managers of the resources, but promoters of children's learning and development.

Summary

Children come to your setting with considerable knowledge of their families, themselves, their languages, their culture. It is important to build on this. Here are some ways in which you can do this:

- Show respect for the languages, cultures, religions, home backgrounds and family value systems of the children and their families.
- Provide opportunities for children to share, take turns and take part in collaborative play.
- Make sure that children are invited to make choices, follow their own interests and get deeply involved in what it is they are doing.
- Organise your resources and the routines of the day so that children become independent and are able to get involved in doing 'real' jobs for real purposes.
- Be prepared to show what you think is worthwhile. Give clear signals about what you think is good and what is not.
- Help children develop an understanding of right and wrong by always giving clear explanations.
- Allow children to express their feelings, even when these are sometimes difficult for you to handle.
- Offer children a cared-for environment and ensure that they do not come across books with pages missing or puzzles with pieces missing.
- Above all, offer a range of meaningful activities so that children can, through first-hand experience, solve problems, communicate with others, express their feelings and understand the social rules.

Communication, language and literacy

You will know that the development of communication, language and literacy is the key to children's learning. Children need to be able to express their thoughts and ideas in speech and in writing, and they need to gain access to the thoughts and ideas of others through listening and reading. Language pervades every activity that children engage in and, since all children are curious, they spend much of their time in the early years trying to understand the symbolic world they encounter. You will remember this from the first chapter of this book.

Two points before we look at the early learning goals. The first is that children learn language and literacy in the same way that they learn about the physical world and the social world. They pay close attention to what those around them are doing and to what they see and hear around them. From this they try to find some pattern which will enable them to work out the rules that apply. Children see print all around them and they begin to wonder what these marks are, why they are there, who made them and for what purpose. They begin making marks for themselves and, at the age of about three (although this varies enormously with experience and exposure to print), they begin to describe these marks sometimes as drawing and sometimes as writing. When children are exposed to books and stories they begin to recognise the links between reading and writing: they understand that the marks can be read and that they always say the same thing. So, children need to see people around them writing and to have examples of writing to look at. They need to have stories and rhymes read to them and to see competent readers using books. They need time to explore these things for themselves, through play and supported by sensitive interaction. This will foster their learning and understanding far better than instructing children in the letters of the alphabet or the patterns of writing.

The second point is that language does not mean only one language, English. Young children will learn most effectively when they are able to build on what they already know. Children who have a language other than English have already acquired this language. They understand how this language works and are able to use it for thinking. Forcing young children to abandon their first language in order to learn English is both insensitive and damaging. Of course young children do need to learn to speak, read and write in English if they are to succeed in the English school system. The argument is that they will best do this where their own language is valued and respected.

The early learning goals for language, literacy and communication

The goals for language, literacy and communication are also grouped and laid out in the same way as those cited earlier.

Set 1: The early learning goals for language for communication

There are six early learning goals for language for communication:

Interact with others, negotiating plans and activities and taking turns in conversation.

Enjoy listening to and using spoken and written language, and readily turn to it in their play and learning.

Sustain attentive listening, responding to what they have heard by relevant comments, questions or actions.

Listen with enjoyment and respond to stories, songs and other music, rhymes and poems and make up their own stories, songs, rhymes and poems.

Extend their vocabulary, exploring the meanings and sounds of new words.

Speak clearly and audibly with confidence and control and show awareness of the listener, for example, by their use of conventions such as greetings, 'please' and 'thank you'.

The first of these early learning goals makes clear the links between speaking and listening and personal, social and emotional development. It also indicates that young children should be in meaningful and often collaborative situations where they have something worth talking about to one another and to the adults. Your setting should be a place where children know that talking to themselves, to one another and to the adults is something that is regarded as worthwhile. There should be opportunities for children to talk about what they are doing, the problems they encounter and the solutions they have come to. Children should be encouraged to talk, but not forced to talk. In schools, children sometimes have to endure something called 'news time' where each child is coerced into saying something about what has happened at home over the weekend. This is both socially divisive (what if all that happened to you at the weekend was to listen to your parents arguing or having to help clean up your younger sibling's mess?) and something that young children find difficult to do. Many adults would hate to be put on the spot like that and have to find something to say in front of others.

In settings where talk has a high profile, children will be talking as they plan and work. They may talk to themselves, to a friend or in a small group. Some of the most confident children may be able to do this in a larger group. As they talk, they will begin to adjust their tone and register to their audience, and this is most successfully developed through role play and drama. Here, where children can take on the roles of others, they can also 'put on' their voices and gestures as they practise being the café manager, the irate mother, the whining baby or the bossy teacher. If you have ever watched a three-year-old playing at being you, you will have been astounded at how much like you this performance is in terms of tone of voice, vocabulary, gestures and body language. Young children are consummate actors as they mimic and exaggerate what they see and hear. As they play and interact, they encounter different models of spoken language, and in an environment rich with meaningful activities they have opportunities to extend their vocabularies. You will see, later in this section, another early learning goal talking of children being able to use language to imagine and create roles.

Think about how children's vocabularies might be enhanced in the following play areas or by visiting the places suggested:

Setting up a clinic or a library or a garage in the classroom or visiting a plant shop or a fire station or the local park.

The rate at which children's vocabulary grows is stunning. When children start in your setting they are usually able to express their needs and desires, to talk about things that are familiar to them and things that matter to them. They have learned all this in their homes and through listening and interaction. Their learning of new words will continue as they are exposed to new and challenging situations and as they encounter new and unfamiliar words in stories read and told.

There used to be the view that adults should use only simple language with young children in order to ensure that they learn new words easily and do not have to cope with what are sometimes considered 'difficult' words. You will have noticed, however, that very young children are often fascinated by long words – things like 'stegosaurus', 'amazing', 'helicopter'. Adults should use normal speech with young children, and this can include long words, complex phrases and technical terms. It is important that when adults use mathematical words, like the names of shapes or words of comparison or position, they use the correct words. Why tell children that bubbles are 'round' when they are, in fact, spherical? Children can learn the word 'sphere' as easily as they can learn the word 'round'. Children who have had a rich diet of hearing stories read and told will benefit in many ways. One of these is the learning of new words; another is the learning of the very specific language found in books. This 'book language' is different in form and style from the language of speech. You would never say something like 'the road was long and winding and the light became dimmer and dimmer as we walked'. You might say, 'we walked down this long road and it was getting dark'. So, the language of books is more complex, more poetic and has its own conventions, using phrases like 'Once upon a time' or 'They all lived happily ever after'. Children need to begin to understand this so that when they begin to make up their own stories they are able to use the language of books in their telling and their writing.

We all want the children we work with to be regarded as polite and acceptable to the adults they encounter, and many of them soon learn the conventional greetings. It is important to remember, however, that there are different ways of greeting and being polite in different cultures. In some cultures it is rude to make eye-to-eye contact. In some cultures thanking is something that is done through the tone of voice. So, sensitivity is called for.

It is of course very important for young children to have as many opportunities to listen and respond to stories, songs, nursery rhymes and poems as possible. In your own setting you will have a wide collection of books in different formats and you will ensure that children can choose to look at and hear books on an individual basis, in a small group or, for the older children, in a large group. Children need to hear new and familiar stories. They need to join in, learning portions or whole texts by heart, and they need to have a go at making up their own stories. They need to be allowed to make their own contributions to the story as they hear it in order that they can link it to their own experience. As children get older they are able to listen for longer and longer periods. Most of all, we want children to have experienced many different genres and to know that stories, songs, rhymes and poems bring with them other worlds to explore in their heads.

Think about the effects of the ways in which Rainbow Playgroup has organised its books into two book corners plus other little book 'holes' into which children may crawl armed with a book or two.

We have many popular children's picture and story books and often have several copies of each available in paperback. We also have some large-format books or Big Books that we use with small groups of children to help them come to understand how books work. We have some information books and some books in English and another language. We don't have enough of those so our aim is to increase the number by the end of this year. We have also made some packs in which we have the book, some story props we have made to go on the magnet board and a tape recording of the story. With the dual-text books we have invited parents in to read the story in the other language. We often use a story as 'a theme' for a few weeks. This term we are using 'The Very Hungry Caterpillar'. We have made a wall story and the children made a caterpillar out of old tights stuffed with newspaper and painted. Then we worked out how to make this caterpillar move by using a pulley, so the caterpillar can crawl through the food and the leaves. The other thing we like to do is to set out a 'small world' scenario with the books. So, with 'Mr Gumpy's Outing', for example, we set up, on a table, a mirror for the lake, a toy boat, toy animals and Lego people together with the book. We noticed that many of the children, especially the bilingual children, would play with this for a long time, retelling the story or making up their own stories.

Now read what they have done at Amandla Early Years Unit and consider the different agenda they have.

We are determined to resist pressure whether it is in the form of insisting on whole-class teaching, introducing synthetic phonics to very young children or anything else that seems to come down from above. This is based on our own understanding that if children are going to not only learn to read but to become readers for life, they must come to know many books and to know that reading is something pleasurable. We invite parents to take home a book on a regular basis and often have meetings with parents to show them how we read with the children. The point we want to make is that we want them to read to the children and not test the children's reading.

We do what we call 'Shared Reading' and this is where we use a Big Book with a small group, and when we have read it we sometimes talk to the children about things like punctuation marks, familiar initial sounds (we try and link these to the children's names), directionality of print, and so on. We do lots and lots of work around rhyme because we know how children hear rhymes and enjoy playing with them and we all believe that they can do this more successfully than hearing the individual sounds of words.

We also have multiple copies of many of the books and sometimes the children play at schools using these.

Set 2: Early learning goals for language for thinking

There are two early learning goals for language for thinking:

Use language to imagine and recreate roles and experiences.

Use talk to organise, sequence and clarify thinking, ideas, feelings and events.

We have talked a little bit about children using language to create and play out roles, and you will be familiar with children doing this. In order to be able to play a role – particularly to play a role in collaboration with others – roles need to be negotiated, play scripts agreed and the action then carried out. It is fascinating to listen to children when they play roles and to hear how they not only use the specific vocabulary related to their role but also adopt tones of voice, gesture, facial expression and intonation patterns very different from their own. This is an impressive range of cognitive skills and one of the best examples of how children use language for thinking.

Ann Browne says:

> Perhaps the most important reason for developing children's oral language is that all learning depends on the ability to question, reason, formulate ideas, pose hypotheses and exchange ideas with others. These are not just oral language skills, they are thinking skills.
>
> (1996, p. 7)

Think about what you have just read and decide whether you agree with what Browne says. Do you think that speaking and listening have a sufficiently high status in your setting?

Good practitioners will be finding ways of helping children develop and refine their skills by making talk an important and valued part of the curriculum. They might invite children to plan aloud what they are going to do; to reflect on what they have done; to share their feelings after a significant experience; to predict what will happen in practical hands-on activities; to relate stories to events or characters in their own lives; to describe and give reasons; to question and answer. You would do well to take time to analyse the place of talk in your curriculum to see whether it is your voice that dominates or whether the children have many and varied opportunities to engage in speaking and listening.

Set 3: Early learning goals for linking sounds and letters

There are three early learning goals for linking sounds and letters. You may want to think about whether you would place these ahead of the learning goals for reading and writing (as they appear in the curriculum guidance) or not.

> **Hear and say initial and final sounds in words, and short vowel sounds within words.**
>
> **Link sounds to letters, naming and sounding the letters of the alphabet.**
>
> **Use their phonic knowledge to write simple regular words and make phonetically plausible attempts at more complex words.**

You will know that there is a move to bring the teaching of phonics into early education despite the repeated efforts of many to stop this happening.

Young children should, certainly, have opportunities to play with letters and sounds, just as they play with objects. They should see examples of the scripts of their language and of the languages of their peers. They may enjoy playing games with initial sounds or making funny alphabet books or thinking about how letters sound. This leads on to the importance of rhyme and rhythm in the early books children are read.

Teaching children how to read is probably the most contentious area in education and continues to be from one decade to another. There are many who believe that children must learn 'the sounds' first, but many, too, who believe that children need to play with books and with language before they can deal with the details of sounds in any meaningful way. Most of those who have had a background in early childhood education are convinced of the fact that children who are learning to read need, more than anything, to be read to. Children who have had positive experiences of being read to are likely to develop an interest in, and sometimes a passion for, books, and, as they get older, may well start to show an interest in aspects of books and of print. They are trying to make sense of the world of print. Some researchers talk about the five aspects or reading:

1   *Literacy awareness*. Through exposure to poems, songs, rhymes and stories, children's attention can be drawn to things like the direction of the print, the differences and similarities between pictures and print, words and letters. They may see someone point to the words as they read – showing one-to-one correspondence.

2   *Syntactic awareness*. Where children have a rich diet of literature they begin to recognise the particular sounds and patterns of the language used in books and, in their own retellings, begin to 'sound like a writer' as they use what is called 'book language'. Many of the books for young children use a highly patterned and repetitive structure that helps the children predict and join in.

3   *Word recognition*. Young children quickly learn to recognise their names and those of family members and friends. Good early years practitioners make much of the names of the children, putting them into stories (in, for example, 'Mr Gumpy's Outing', where instead of animals, some children go on the boat); making up stories about individual children; writing out the words of songs with children's names in ('There was a farmer had a dog and Benny was his name, oh!').

4   *Phonological awareness*. This is the ability to hear and identify sound patterns. There is a considerable body of research evidence (some of this cited by Dombey (1999)) which shows that young children find it difficult to split a spoken word into its component phonemes or sounds. They find it even harder to blend the sounds to make the whole word. They find the initial sound quite easy, the last sound not too difficult, but the middle sound almost impossible. Because rhyme plays such an important

part in the culture of young children, practitioners who use rhyme help children work out words using the initial sound/phoneme (or 'onset') and the rest of the syllable or word (or rime). In the word 'hat', for example, the onset is 'h' and the rime is 'at'. Children find this much simpler than identifying all three phonemes, 'h', 'a', 't'. Goswami (1993) has shown that where children encounter rhymes they can use analogy (spotting patterns) to help them work out new words. So, a child who has learned about hat and cat will find 'mat' easy to read. There is also evidence to show that children play with language just as they play with anything else they are trying to make sense of, and in this play rhyming plays a large part. So, good early years practitioners will spend a considerable amount of time playing with initial sounds, clapping out the syllables and making up rhymes. Many of the skipping, clapping songs help children identify and pay attention to syllables. Young children also enjoy making up alliterative sentences – sentences in which each word starts with the same letter ('exciting Ellie eats elephants'; 'brave Bilal bites bananas').

5   *Orthographic awareness.* This involves labelling the letters of the alphabet and is something that many parents are keen to see their children do. Children enjoy chanting the alphabet and may look at alphabet friezes. They may pay attention to the letter at the start of their name and enjoy playing with magnetic letters.

It needs to be re-emphasised that all of this needs to take place in the context of story and play. Decontextualised activities like flashcards and worksheets will not foster children's learning and development. Although the children may show short-term gains (and you might do well here to remember the work of Katz and Elkind referred to in Chapter 1), there may be long-term damage to their dispositions to learn.

The next set of early learning goals relate to reading. When you look at them, keep in mind what you have just read and remember that, in helping children become readers, familiarity with a range of written forms, play with rhyme, alliteration and syllable, knowledge of the alphabet and opportunities to make analogies and talk about their findings will be more helpful than simple decoding practice.

Set 4: The early learning goals for reading

There are five early learning goals for reading:

Explore and experiment with sounds, words and texts.

Re-tell narratives in the correct sequence, drawing on language patterns of stories.

Read a range of familiar and common words and simple sentences independently.

Know that print carries meaning and, in English, is read from left to right and top to bottom.

Show an understanding of the elements of stories, such as main character, sequence of events, and openings, and how information can be found in non-fiction texts to answer questions about where, who, why and how.

Good early years classes offer many opportunities for children to have stories read to them, to make up their own stories, to think and talk about what happens in the stories and to play with sounds and words. In terms of helping children make up their own stories, songs and rhymes you may want to consider how often it is through role-play that children invent scenarios and characters. They try on roles and voices and gestures and build their own play scripts which involve orchestrating who is who and what is happening – a story in the making. Practitioners who are skilled storytellers use different voices and props and sometimes let the children take charge of how the story develops. They know that children who have a story told and read are fortunate in coming to understand that it is the print in the book version that makes the story exactly the same each time it is read. In terms of becoming a reader this is an important lesson to learn.

Think about what the following set of examples say about how you can enhance your provision to make your young pupils more likely to become readers and writers for life.

Hannah, aged four, talked about stories with happy endings and reflected that in all those she had come across there was a bad character. Her developing understanding of the conventions of stories led her to consider good over-coming evil.

'This is a book written by Roald Dahl, with pictures by Quentin Blake,' the adult said. The child, aged five, asked, 'Don't you mean "illustrated by Quentin Blake"?'

Sukvinder, aged three, tells her mum the story of 'Goldilocks and the Three Bears': 'Daddy Bear, Mummy Bear and Baby Bear and a little girl came and she ate the porridge and she broke the chair and she went to bed and she went home and that's the end.'

Ben wants someone to read him the instructions that came with a set of magnets. 'Do they tell you how they work?'

Here are some ideas which may help you improve what you currently offer for children both in terms of resources and of an ethos of literacy. We might call this a recipe for a book-friendly setting.

1   Provide information books for children to explore. Ensure that they are attractive and inviting.
2   Read aloud recipes, planting instructions, etc. in context. For example, if you are planting seeds, read what it says on the seed packet.
3   Make books available to support ongoing and meaningful activities. This makes them a natural and integral part of the learning environment.
4   Talk to children about books – not only about details like 'front' and 'back' and 'cover', but also about the sometimes deep and difficult themes in books. *Not Now, Bernard* is about a child being ignored by his parents; *Mine* is about jealousy; *The Sad Book* is about death. It is important to talk to children about the main characters and invite them to talk about what these characters are like.
5   Welcome children's popular culture (television, film, video, pop music) into the classroom and use these as themes to promote literacy.

There is no doubt that some children will have had enough experience of activities associated with speaking and listening, reading and writing, to be able to read by the time they leave the reception class. Children who have been immersed in stories and book language and who have played with alliteration and rhyme are likely to find reading immensely rewarding and go on to be readers. But there are many children who still fear that reading is difficult and that they will fail. Approaches to reading which 'test' children often result in fear of failure. Confidence, self-esteem and enjoyment are prerequisites for becoming readers.

Do remember that writers of good books for children play with language in ways that help children read. What is more, this is done in the context of something that is exciting or funny or sad. First of all the children are drawn into the story and then they are drawn into the text. And as they hear the story again and again they are able to join in and predict and, eventually, to read.

Consider these sentences taken from some well-known children's books.

My old Teddy's leg came off. Poor old Teddy!
I took him to the Teddy doctor. She made Teddy better.
My old Teddy's leg came off. Poor old Teddy.
I took him to the Teddy doctor. She made Teddy better.

                (D. Mansell, 'My Old Teddy')

Here's a little baby
One, two, three
Stands in his cot
What does he see?
(Janet and Allen Ahlberg, 'Peepo')

. . . Auntie, Auntie Bibba.
Auntie Bibba came inside with her
Arms wide, wide, wide
And one big, big smile.
'Oooh!' she said.
'I want to squeeze him,
I want to squeeze the baby,
I want to squeeze him
SO MUCH!'

        (Trish Cooke, 'So Much')

You don't have here the wonderful pictures that extend and enhance the texts, but even from these brief extracts you can see the devices used by good authors: humour, repetition, rhythm, rhyme, using children's experience and interests. Immersion in books like these, together with talk about authors and illustrators, characters and words, will make reading possible and satisfying for all children.

Set 5: The early learning goals for writing

There are three early learning goals for writing, and one also refers to a learning goal relating to sounds and letters:

Attempt writing for different purposes using features of different forms such as lists, stories and instructions.

Use their phonic knowledge to write simple regular words and make phonetically plausible attempts at more complex words.

> Write their own names and other things such as labels and captions
> and begin to form simple sentences, sometimes using punctuation.

Young children begin to write as part of their exploration of their physical world. Making marks with a finger on a misted window pane or with a stick in the sand, children begin to realise that their hands themselves, or a tool used as an extension of their hands, can leave a trace. Once children are offered pencils or crayons they discover that the marks they make are permanent. This is a satisfying event and one children are keen to repeat – often with disastrous consequences for walls and floors! Children's earliest marks are not representations of anything, but a record of their physical movements. But as children see people around them engaged in writing, they begin to want to discover what it is that these people are doing. So, their own mark-making becomes more intentional and the intention is often to communicate some meaning.

When children enter your setting they are often able to say that their marks are either drawings or writing. In other words, they recognise the differences between two symbolic systems – a significant achievement in itself. In their earliest attempts at writing they will often include writing-like patterns and letter-like shapes. Do remember that children who have seen adults using Bengali script, for example, will include Bengali letter-like shapes in their writing. This, again, is evidence of children's knowledge and not of their lack of knowledge. As children see more modelling of writing and as they see writing in books, in the setting and in the world around them, their attempts at writing will move closer and closer to recognisable letters. Often the first letters you will recognise will be the letters in the child's name. It is worth paying close attention to what it is the children are doing as they write and it is important to remember that writing is more difficult than reading since it involves the skills of actually forming the letters, words and sentences as well as making up the meaning.

Children are not only working out how the written system works, but also trying to understand the different functions and purposes for writing. They see adults around them engaged in acts of writing for different purposes – a note to the milkman, an entry in a diary, a message on the message board, a letter to Gran, a form in the post office, and so on. In your setting you should try to offer children opportunities to explore the purposes of writing in as many meaningful ways as possible.

Think about what staff at Rainbow Playgroup say about how they are encouraging children to explore the purposes of writing:

Well, first we set up a writing corner. We put up alphabet charts in three languages (English, Bengali and Turkish). We put in an old typewriter, a stapler, a hole punch, pairs of scissors, lots of different sizes and types of pencils, crayons, coloured pencils and felt-tipped pens. We put out small books of blank pages stapled together, writing paper, strips of paper, envelopes and blank forms. The children often go in there and do their own writing. We notice that they always write in the boxes of the blank forms.

We timetable ourselves so that one of us is always in the writing corner, sometimes writing our letters or shopping lists. The children are always interested in what we are doing and want to have a go themselves.

We try and think of what examples of and opportunities for writing we can put in our imaginative play areas. Last term we had a café and the children helped us make signs for the café. We wrote up a menu and there were little notebooks for the children to use when they took an order. There were strips of paper for them to use for the bills. One member of staff brought in a credit card and the children had fun making up secret numbers and learning to 'sign' their bills. One of the children suggested we had a recipe book so the cook would know what to cook, and so the children made their own recipe book which included pictures and their attempts at writing or our writing when they wanted us to write for them.

Think about this:

The Beckham Children's Centre visited Rainbow Playgroup to look at its provision and added the following ideas, thinking particularly about providing for the learning needs of the children in the reception classes:

> We read Nigel Hall's work about play and literacy and decided to set up a garage in the classroom. We visited a garage and the children helped us decide how to set it up, what notices to write, and then we intervened. We told the children that if they wanted to play in the garage they had to apply, and that led to a discussion about what it meant to apply. Drawing on Hall's work, we worked with the children to devise a job advert and a job description, and the children then filled in the forms we designed. The forms required basic information – things like name and address and phone number plus providing a space where children were asked to write 'Why you would be good at this job'. Children all enjoyed designing the adverts and forms and filled them in well, giving us an idea of what they could write unaided.

In order to plan for and promote early writing, it is important to understand something of what is known about how young children make sense of print as they attempt to do it for themselves. Writing is a complex thing: it involves both deciding what to write (which is called composition) and knowing how to make the relevant marks on paper (which is called transcription). Transcription involves children knowing something about how to form the letters (what we call 'handwriting') and how to spell the actual words and put them down on the paper. So, it involves working out the rules of spelling and of grammar (things like capital letters, punctuation, spaces between words). You may have children come and ask you to write something for them, such as 'write "I love you, Mummy" or "Come to my house to play"'. And you may have seen children making marks on paper that they call writing (as opposed to drawing) and revealing their developing concepts about the written system. A child may move from strings of letter-like shapes to rows of letters (often drawn from their names) to words made up of initial and last sound (I LV U) to some correctly spelled words combined with abbreviated forms. Children experiment with capital and lower-case letters and often incorporate punctuation marks in their writing.

As with all other aspects of learning, children see experienced writers writing and they see writing in the environment – on television, products, in books and magazines, etc. They have a go at making similar marks for themselves and later say that these marks 'say something'. There are many books and articles about this early writing, and there is no room in this book to go into this in any detail. It is important, though, that children have opportunities for writing, that they see others writing, that they are encouraged to have a go and that, as they get older and more aware of the relationships between letters, sounds and words, they do not lose the confidence to try for themselves.

Set 6: Early learning goals for handwriting

There is just one early learning goal for handwriting:

Use a pencil and hold it effectively to form recognisable letters most of which are formed correctly.

Summary
- Language pervades every area of learning.
- Children learn language and literacy as active learners trying to understand the world they inhabit.
- Children who have already acquired a language other than English should be supported in using this language as they acquire English.
- A good nursery or playgroup is one where children and adults know that talking is respected and valued.
- Adults should use appropriate language which is aimed to help children understand and to move on in their learning.
- Books introduce children to wider worlds and increased vocabulary as well as the very specific language of books.

continued on next page

- All young children should have access to books, rhymes, songs and stories on a regular basis individually and in small groups.
- Children should have opportunities to retell known stories and to make up their own stories. Adults should try telling stories as well as reading them.
- Adults should help children come to understand how books work by drawing their attention to the direction of print, inviting them to turn pages, helping them focus on the print itself and begin to realise that it is people who write and illustrate books.
- Adults can help children find the patterns in language by spending some considerable time reading and creating rhymes, singing songs and encouraging children to play with spoken and written language.
- Adults should, above all, help children realise that, in reading, the task is to lift the writer's meaning from the page. They should help children use all means available to them to understand and then retell the story.
- Adults can introduce children to many aspects of literacy by including children's names in stories, songs, rhymes and games. Children's names are significant to them, and using them offers many opportunities for children to learn about letters and sounds.
- Adults should display alphabets and scripts in the languages of the children and should offer children magnetic letters to play with.
- Adults should ensure that they provide many opportunities for children to explore reading and writing through familiar and meaningful situations.
- Adults should model both reading and writing, showing children how expert readers and writers operate.
- Adults should pay close attention to what the children do as they play at reading and writing and use this to inform their planning.
- Adults need to remember that writing is a complex skill and be willing to 'scribe' for the children.

Chapter 6

Understanding and explaining the physical world

Dov (aged four) arrives at the playgroup and hangs his coat on his peg. He then goes over to the book corner and spends about twenty minutes sorting out the books in one of the book boxes. An adult (who has decided to observe Dov for that morning) notices that he is making piles of books of the same size. Satisfied with that, he goes over to the junk modelling area and sorts out some things he wants to use. He selects an empty box and a yoghurt carton, together with some brightly coloured wrapping paper. He spends the next hour or so attempting to wrap up his chosen boxes. He manages to wrap the box by placing it in the centre of a large piece of paper and folding the paper so that the entire box is hidden. He fastens the paper down using sticky tape. The yoghurt carton causes him more difficulty. He attempts to cover it in the same way as the box, but the shape is difficult for him to manage. The worker notices that he keeps picking up the yoghurt carton and examining it, and each time he does this he cuts the wrapping paper. Observing that he will not be successful in his chosen task, the worker offers him help, which he accepts. Happy with his wrapped boxes, he joins three girls in the construction area and watches what they are doing. He then carefully selects some blocks and proceeds to build a wall. The worker notices that in doing this he starts off using blocks of the same length, but when he runs out of those on the second layer of his wall, he resorts to using two smaller blocks, which are equivalent to one large block. At tidying-up time he joins the girls in carefully stacking the blocks in the correct place. The stencils of the shapes of the blocks placed on the shelves help him to match them. In his story group he happily joins in with the songs, and the worker notices that when they are singing counting songs, Dov is using his fingers to count on. It is Dov's turn to set the tables for lunch and he is very efficient at setting the table for five children and one adult.

After reading this, think about what you can now say that Dov knows about mathematics. Think about things like counting and exploring space and all the aspects of mathematics you are aware of.

Dov, like most children of his age, has already learned a great deal about counting, matching, sorting, estimating, shape and space, patterns and solving problems. He has learned much of this at home in the everyday activities which involve mathematics.

Here is what Dov's key worker wrote in her analysis of what he knew:

> Dov can sort and match according to size and shape. He is able to estimate area and used his eye to check on the size of the box and the size of the paper. He understands that two smaller blocks are equal in length to one long block. He knows a lot of number songs and uses his fingers to count on. He understands about one-to-one correspondence and was able to set the table with one fork, one knife, one spoon, one table mat and one cup for each person. He also knows that the adult setting requires larger utensils.

You may want to read that through again and highlight the words which you may regard as mathematical words.

Mathematics is a word that continues to strike terror in the hearts of many childcare and nursery practitioners and even in the hearts of many teachers who have had to upgrade their own mathematical knowledge in order to be recognised as teachers. It is perhaps this that has persuaded curriculum developers to talk of problem-solving, reasoning and numeracy in the proposed Early Years Foundation Stage. Yet the reality is that we use mathematics all the time in our everyday lives. What is interesting is that we are often unaware that we are using mathematics.

Here is a small activity for you to try.

Write down all the things you have done this week which involved mathematics.

Did you come up with any of these things:

- put up shelves;
- made sure you were on the correct bus;
- worked out how much time you needed to make a journey;
- put a casserole in the oven for an hour and twenty minutes;
- checked you had been given the correct change;
- measured your child to record her growth;
- wrapped a parcel;
- followed a knitting pattern;
- cut a slice of bread in half?

Most of us are able to do these things without difficulty, just as we are able to pick up a pencil or turn on the television. Yet all of them involve the skills and knowledge we call mathematics.

In the Foundation Stage, mathematical knowledge is regarded as being important, and practitioners are encouraged to help children explore the world and to use mathematics as a tool for exploration and for explaining what is noticed. What is emphasised is that children should be able to enjoy acquiring mathematical knowledge and that this is most likely to happen when they do so through purposeful or meaningful activities. Children who are involved in cooking can see the point of weighing and counting. Children turning the home corner into the cottage of the three bears can see the point of exploring size. You, as practitioners, are charged with enabling children to be confident and able not only to solve problems but also to know *how* they did so. You are also tasked with helping children to be able to use mathematical language in their play. Your role in this is vital, and if you are able to become more confident about your own knowledge of mathematics, this will engender confidence and enjoyment in the children.

In the Foundation Stage, children are expected to invent, use and understand numerals and to perform operations with numbers; they explore pattern, shape, space and measures. Just as in all other areas of learning, children should be involved in first-hand practical experience in meaningful contexts. The adults working with them should strive to use the correct mathematical language to help children use this very specific language themselves to describe and explain the processes they are involved in.

Mathematics is an area of learning which is not necessarily dependent on understanding and speaking English. In lifelike contexts, where the meaning is embedded in the activity, children who have English as an additional language will be able to engage in problem-solving activities alongside their English-speaking peers. This is only true if the children can see the purpose of any activity or select to use the materials on offer in a way which meets their needs and interests.

Think about some of the activities you offer which would include some opportunities for problem-solving, reasoning and numeracy and where the context itself would make it possible for children with little or no English to become as involved as others.

Here are some responses to this question from practitioners:

In exploring floating and sinking with the children I introduced two hoops and invited the children first to guess or predict which of their chosen objects would float or sink and place the object in the appropriate hoop. Then the children put the objects in water and noticed what happened. Then they again put the objects in the hoops, but when one or two objects were found to do 'both' or to float first and then sink, the children couldn't decide where to put them. When I made the hoops overlap a little so that a Venn diagram was made, the children quickly put their objects in the 'both' category.

We often do cooking or sometimes just make sandwiches, but these activities are always full of possibilities for the language of maths. I find myself saying things like 'Let's cut it in half' or 'Shall we cut them diagonally?' or 'Do you want the thick or the thinner slice?', and so on. And because you can eat the result, all the children are keen to get involved.

The early learning goals for mathematics (problem-solving, reasoning and numeracy)

Set 1: The early learning goals that relate to using numbers as labels and for counting

There are four early leaning goals for mathematics.

Say and use number names in order in familiar contexts.

Count reliably up to ten everyday objects.

Recognise numerals 1 to 9.

Use developing mathematical ideas and methods to solve practical problems.

Most young children use number names in their everyday conversation. They talk about their age, attempt to count, memorise number songs and certainly understand small numbers when it comes to getting something nice – like sweets or cakes. With experience, their understanding of numbers increases and their use of number names becomes more accurate. Similarly, children start counting objects in their play, often inaccurately at first. Again, with support and experience they become more accurate.

Just as you would ensure that you have alphabets displayed in your room, so you would want to have a number line and, if at all possible, a number line for the number symbols in other languages. You would also want to ensure that you have magnetic numerals and numbers displayed where relevant and appropriate. Children see numerals around them – on buses, on television, on their front doors and in shops. They are often interested to know what these say and will even include numerals in their own mark-making. Some numbers are significant to children, and the most obvious ones relate to their ages. Pat Gura gives a lovely example of three-year-old Sean exploring how to represent his exact age of three and a half:

In a group of children aged three to six who were talking about their ages and examining a set of numerals, Sean selected the numeral '3' and placed it on the magnet board:

[. . . The adult commented] 'Three. That's good. Now what about the half? Shall I show you how to do that?' (Sean nods. Andrew and Joshua move closer.) Next to Sean's three, the adult creates the symbol for 'half' with three pieces: 'There you are, Sean. Now it says three and a half.' Sean is very pleased but Joshua is enthralled. He promptly copies the three and a half, telling anyone who cares to listen: 'That says three and a half'. Then, announcing each one as he goes along, he makes four and a half, eight and a half, nought and a half, nine and a half, two and a half. At this point he stops and reads them all back.

(1996, p. 150)

It is interesting to note that children in the Foundation Stage are not required to record numbers. An understanding of how numbers work and the ability to recognise the symbols is what matters.

Think about what the example below tells you about how a particular interest can lead a child into deeper exploration than is suggested by the early learning goals.

In her play, five-year-old Hannah decided to make a measuring chart. She got four pieces of paper and stuck them together. She then started at the bottom of the page with number one and went up the page creating a totally accurate number line. She wrote the numbers correctly up to 137 and then went on to measure herself, her brother, her best friend, two dolls and a toy lion.

Those working with young children will use number songs, rhymes, stories and games as part of their daily provision. Most children coming to your setting will already know some number songs and rhymes. These may be in English or in the languages spoken at home. Young children greatly enjoy singing such songs and chanting rhymes, particularly when they are brought to life either through using props on a magnet or a felt board, or by using the children themselves to 'act' out the song. A familiar example is getting children to 'be' the five little speckled frogs. It is worth building up your collection of number rhymes and songs and inviting parents and carers to teach you songs and rhymes you don't yet know and which may be in the languages spoken by the children. And you may want to record these on to tapes so that the children can choose to listen to them when you are not available to sing them. Making Big Books of these songs and rhymes provides an invaluable resource and brings to life the links between literacy and mathematics.

Think about how many of these songs you know and consider how you might do any or all of the following:

- *invite the children to act them out;*
- *make them into a Big Book;*
- *make story props for the magnet board;*
- *anything else?*

One, two, three, four, five
Once I caught a fish alive . . .

One, two, buckle my shoe . . .

Two, four, six, eight,
Mary at the garden gate . . .

Five elephants went out to play
On a spider's web one day . . .

Five currant buns in the baker's shop . . .

Five little speckled frogs sat on a speckled log . . .

There were six little frogs
Sitting on a well . . .

When Goldilocks went to the house of the bears
Oh what did her blue eyes see? . . .

Five little monkeys jumping on the bed
One fell off and banged his head . . .

Stories are another invaluable source for mathematical ideas and concepts. If you take the time to look through some of the books and stories you know well, you will find mathematics embedded in the stories. There are many attractive counting books, and children may well be interested in these, and you should certainly ensure that you have some. But just as reading is about more than simply decoding the words, understanding of mathematical concepts comes more through exploring these concepts in situations that children understand than through merely chanting them.

Think about how you might use each of the stories below to enhance children's use of mathematical language and understanding of mathematical concepts:

- Where's Spot?
- Titch
- The Three Billy Goats Gruff
- What's the Time, Mr Wolf?
- Mr Gumpy's Outing.

You will realise that *Where's Spot?* offers opportunities for talking about the language of position, using words like 'under', 'inside', 'behind', and so on. *Titch* and *The Three Billy Goats* offer opportunities for thinking about size and about comparison – tall, taller, tallest. Many of the books written for children are rich in possibilities for exploring aspects of number and mathematics.

Finally in this section, it is worth thinking about stories you can make up to explore different mathematical concepts. In doing this you should also think of what props you can introduce so that in the telling of your story you give the children physical support for the concepts. Hilary Faust, an early years mathematics consultant, has made up many such stories and she insists that after the telling of the story, the props be left out for the children to play with as they retell the story or create their own story. One of her stories concerns a teddy bear who decides to send his cousin a birthday present. He finds a small bowl (which Hilary shows to the children) and then looks for a box to put the bowl in. Hilary has a collection of boxes, some of which are too small and some of which are too big. There is only one which is 'just right'. You can find this and other mathematical stories in *Animated Stories for Young Mathematicians* by Hilary Faust and can find details of how to buy this at http://www.beam.co.uk.

Games are another way of helping children understand number concepts. There are many commercially produced games and you will want to examine them to ensure that they will be relevant and meaningful to the children and that they do not reflect images which are monocultural or even offensive. BEAM (whose website is given above) has a wide selection of number games which are relevant to children in the Foundation Stage. There are also the traditional games of hopscotch, skipping games, finger plays, circle games and ball/bat/hoop games. In these, the players (including the adults) share the agreed rules and can only change them by negotiating.

You can also make games, and when you do you can ensure that they meet the learning needs you have identified from your observations of the children. Some of the best games derive from the stories you read. Here is an example to illustrate this:

Jenny, one of the nursery nurses in a reception class, noticed that some of the children were interested in large numbers. She decided to make a game based on a popular picture book, *Not Now Bernard* by David McKee. The game was essentially a number line and the children had to throw the dice and move the number of steps indicated by the number on the dice. The number line moved from Bernard being ignored by his parents to the monster ending up in Bernard's bed and the number line went from 1 to 100.

The children who played the game did so with enthusiasm, initially always with an adult present but later on they were able to play on their own. After a few weeks, Jenny decided that the children might need some cognitive challenge and so she added some labels to the number line in the form of pictures of the monster roaring. Each time the child landed on one of these pictures she or he had to go backwards rather than forwards the number of steps indicated on the dice. In this way she was helping the children explore both counting on and counting down.

Set 2: The early learning goals connected with calculating

There are four early leaning goals connected with calculating:

> In practical activities and discussion begin to use the vocabulary involved in adding and subtracting.
>
> Use language such as 'more' and 'less' to compare two numbers.
>
> Find one more or one less than a number from one to ten.
>
> Begin to relate addition to combining two groups of objects and subtraction to 'taking away'.

Through practical activities, games, songs, rhymes, stories and discussion, children start exploring what happens when things are added to or taken away from something. Many children have experience of this in their real lives, as when they ask for 'one more' or when Mum says, 'If you don't share I will take it away.'

Think about what these activities show about children's developing understanding of calculation.

Rosie and Shameela are in the home corner, setting the table. Rosie counts out the chairs: 'One, two, three, four.' She counts the dolls: 'One, two, three.' Then she says to Shameela, 'Get another chair, Sham. We need five and there's only four here.'

Anneka and Liam are setting the table for lunch. Liam puts out seven place mats and Anneka tells him to take one away because there are only six children at that table.

Zubeida says, 'If you give me one more I will have more than Tommy.'

Paulina and Dean are playing a game using dice. Pauline throws a three and then a two. 'Three and two: that makes five, so I can move five places.' The nursery nurse asked: 'How did you work that out, Paulina? Did you start with three and count on like this?'

Abi, Darren and Charlotte are handing out slices of orange at circle time. Charlotte turns to the adult and says, 'I need two more pieces for me and Morwen.'

During a singing session six children are at the front, pretending to be frogs. Bobby suddenly shouts out, 'If Marcus and Valya sit down there will be four left.' The teacher asked, 'How did you work that out, Bobby?' And Bobby replied, 'I counted six on my fingers and then put two fingers down and I had four left.'

It is useful to think carefully about what you, as practitioner, would have said, noted or done to consolidate and enhance learning. Here are some responses to consider:

I would have said to Rosie something like 'Wow, Rosie. You are very clever to have worked out that you need one more chair to have five.'

In the example of Abi and his friends at circle time I would have asked Charlotte how she worked out that she needed two more pieces. I think it is important to get children to think about how they arrived at solutions.

The role of the adult in all of this is to ensure comprehension and enhance learning by using the correct mathematical language with the children; posing problems when reading stories or chanting songs; showing an interest in how the children arrived at an answer or a solution; and providing opportunities for games and for addition and subtraction in role-play areas.

Set 3: The early learning goals related to pattern, shape, space and measures

There are five early learning goals related to pattern, shape, space and measures:

Use language such as 'greater', 'smaller', 'heavier' or 'lighter' to compare quantities.

Talk about, recognise and recreate simple patterns.

Use language such as 'circle' or 'bigger' to describe the shape and size of solids and flat shapes.

Use everyday words to describe position.

Use developing mathematical ideas and methods to solve practical problems.

Think about the mathematical words you can list relating to pattern, to shape and to position.

You may have come up with words like 'circle', 'square', 'big', 'small', 'more', 'less' and 'equals'. The language of mathematics includes words relating to everyday life, and you may be surprised to discover just how many of them you use without even realising this. You will discover more about this in the section about physical development.

Consider this example:

Three children are playing on the outdoor climbing frame.

SUNITA: I'm climbing right to the top. I am higher than you.
SORAYA: I can climb even higher. See, I'm the very highest.
PRIYA: I am coming next to you then I'll also be the very highest.
SUNITA: Let's go across here. You can follow me. I am going first and then you, Priya, and you last [points to Soraya]. Then we can go underneath and hang down.

You may want to have a go at underlining the words you think relate to mathematics in that example. Here are some of the words underlined by a group of teachers and childcare practitioners in a workshop: top, higher, highest, next to, across, first, last, underneath, down. Did any of those words surprise you? You will see that the children, in their play, were using mathematical language to describe comparisons of height and also to explore position and direction.

Some practitioners, on reading this outcome, may decide that it would be beneficial to teach children mathematical terms through decontextualised activities – like asking children to colour all the circles on a worksheet red and all the triangles blue. Compare this type of activity which involves the child in merely following instructions with a self-chosen activity where the child is involved in physically exploring the properties of shapes – as in painting, drawing, selecting materials to make a model. Think, too, about what you know about the importance for young children of seeing the purpose of what they are doing. Is there a real purpose – one that would make sense to a child – in colouring things in according to instructions, or is this merely something the child has been told to do?

Piaget talks of two different types of knowledge that children use when they act on objects. He called these 'physical knowledge' (which relates to what children discover about objects they handle) and 'logicomathematical knowledge' (which relates to what children discover when they make comparisons between objects). For Piaget, physical knowledge comes from information external to the child – from the direct physical exploration of the objects. The source of logicomathematical knowledge is internal: it is what happens inside the child's head. It is important to note that, for Piaget, the two are intertwined and the child cannot separate out one type of knowledge from another. A child comes to recognise the colour red by comparing objects of different colours and by classifying them. No child is able to classify objects without a great deal of experience of exploring them using both his or her senses and physical exploration of objects. The children on the climbing frame in the example above are physically exploring space and position and have obviously explored these concepts before. Through their physical and sensory explorations they have come to understand the concepts of higher and highest. In order for children to develop the language of mathematics they need to explore the physical properties of objects in order to classify, sort, match, sequence and count. It is only through doing this in situations that are personally meaningful to them that they are able to internalise the concepts so that they are later able to use this language with understanding.

Think about the activities described below and see if you can identify just what it is about them that allows them to be called 'meaningful'. Think, too, about which aspects of mathematics the child might explore and about how the adults involved and planned and provided for this.

The children are baking cookies. Each child has a bowl and a spoon, and the adult has written the recipe out in large script and reads it aloud as she helps the children in the process. There are six children in the group and the adult has a cookie tin with twelve sections.

The class has read the story 'The Three Bears' and the staff have rearranged the home corner so that it has become the bears' cottage. In the home corner are three chairs of different sizes, three beds of different sizes and three bowls of different sizes.

All the children take turns to help set the tables for lunch each day. They have to set a place for each of six children and an additional place for the adult. Each place has a knife, a fork, a spoon and a glass. The children's utensils are smaller than those for the adult.

In the garden the staff have set up a bus station and have put a number on each of the cars and bikes.

The theme in the reception class is the story of 'Jack and the Beanstalk'. The home corner has been turned into the Giant's Castle and contains a giant bowl and a giant spoon. The beanstalk goes from floor to ceiling.

One of the things that young children do as they come to understand the world is to try to find the patterns in things they encounter. These can be the patterns relating to language, as we saw in an earlier chapter, or the patterns they see in tiles or wallpaper or in mathematics. Mathematics, which is a symbolic way of explaining and describing aspects of the physical world, is highly dependent on pattern and on rules. We classify and sort things according to what features they have in common. A child playing with six wooden blocks – four red and two blue, for example – might sort them according to colour or might line them up in a pattern – two red, one blue, two red, one blue – or might even just divide them into two equal piles. As in all early learning, young children need to see patterns in their world and to create and recreate them according to their own interests.

Think about what these two examples show about what aspects of mathematics the children are exploring:

The children are at a table threading beads. Each child has been given a card which shows a pattern of beads and has been asked to copy that pattern.

Four children in the block play area have constructed a 'building' and have used cylindrical blocks separated out by small cubes. The adult watching them comments, 'I like the pattern you have used – cylinder, cube, cylinder, cube.'

Young children in your setting will already be using their developing mathematical understanding to solve practical problems. You have only to observe children playing in the home corner or the outdoor play space or the construction or creative areas to notice how often they do this. Re-read the example of Dov at the beginning of this chapter to see just how many practical problems Dov solved in his play.

Gréco (1962) gives a fascinating example of just how important it is to let children actually solve problems for themselves rather than giving them 'fake' problems to solve. How many of you, I wonder, can still remember some of the meaningless mathematical problems you encountered at school – problems of the type 'If John has seventeen liquorice sticks and twelve sherbet lemons and his sister has twice as many liquorice sticks and half the number of sherbet lemons, how many sweets does his sister have?'

> Gréco's example concerned a five-year-old boy called Jean-Pierre who lived with his mother, father and sibling. Jean Pierre could count to thirty. Each day his mother asked him to put out the table napkins for the main meal of the day. On the first day Jean Pierre took out one napkin and put it on one plate. He then returned to the cupboard in order to get the second napkin which he put on the second plate. In all he made four trips in order to match each napkin to each plate. About three months later he decided to count the plates and then counted out four napkins. This continued for six days.
>
> On the seventh day there was a guest for dinner and Jean Pierre found an additional plate on the table. He took out four napkins as usual, but then realised that there was a plate without a napkin. Dismayed by this, he returned all four napkins to the cupboard and started all over again, this time making five trips to and from the table. The next day the guest was no longer there, but Jean Pierre made four trips to the table and he kept up this method for five more days, when he returned to his previous method of counting plates and counting napkins. Ten days later he was told that there was to be a guest for dinner again. This time he counted out his four napkins and then returned to the cupboard to get an extra one for the guest. And on the following day when it was only the family for dinner he calmly counted out four plates and four napkins. The presence of guests for dinner never again disturbed his counting system.
>
> (Gréco 1962, p. 25)

Summary

- Children learn about mathematical concepts through their everyday experiences as they try to understand the world in which they live.
- Children entering your setting have already learned a great deal about counting, matching, sorting, classifying, ordering, comparing and sequencing. They have also learned about pattern, shape, space and measures.
- Mathematics is embedded in most of the activities of everyday life. Practitioners should try to be more alert to the mathematical potential of everyday activities.
- Children who have a language other than English can explore mathematical concepts without being dependent on understanding or speaking English.
- Children should encounter numerous opportunities to explore objects and to be involved in first-hand experience. This will allow them to move to the stage where they are no longer dependent on handling objects because they can hold concepts in their heads.
- The use of mathematical language is an important part of development.
- Children should be helped by adults to acquire the specific language of mathematics, and adults should listen attentively to children to discover just how much they understand.
- Adults should show a genuine interest in how children have solved problems.
- Offering children opportunities to explore mathematical concepts in meaningful situations will help children both to build on what they already know and to move ahead in their learning.
- Songs, rhymes, games and stories provide an invaluable resource for the development of mathematical concepts and language.
- Opportunities should be provided for children to explore shape, space and pattern.
- Numerals should be displayed and children invited to examine and explore these.
- Just as names are significant to children, so are ages. Practitioners should explore possibilities for building on children's interest in their ages (and sometimes those of their friends and family members).
- Practitioners should offer children opportunities to think and to solve problems, rather than giving them recipes or solutions. In this way children are allowed to be inventive and thoughtful, and to develop confidence in their own abilities to solve problems they encounter in their play and learning.

Physical development

You will know, from your own experience, how young children really need to be physically active as they learn and play. One of the most damaging features of children starting formal schooling very young is that they are required to be seated, often indoors, for long periods of time. The Foundation Stage now offers those working with children in the reception class the structure for finding ways for these children, in parallel with younger children in all settings, to have ongoing access to some outdoor area where they are able to develop the skills of running, jumping, balancing, climbing, riding small vehicles, pushing, pulling, catching, throwing, sliding, and so on. Young children's physical skills develop rapidly and they enjoy their developing prowess which gives them greater and greater control over their environment. Children's fine motor skills also develop rapidly, particularly where they are given free access to a range of tools, objects, construction materials and malleable materials to explore.

Practitioners should plan activities that offer physical challenges, that are imaginative and enjoyable, and they should allow children the time and the space in which to develop their skills. Children should have as many varied experiences to explore the physical world as it is possible to provide. Physical development is inseparable from other aspects of development, and a good early years setting will ensure that a broad curriculum is on offer indoors and out. Outdoors it is possible to offer activities and experiences on a larger scale than indoors, and this provides children with opportunities to compare, to explore in different dimensions and to refine their understanding.

Resourcing the outdoor play space is something that requires ingenuity rather than money. Natural and found objects provide open-ended resources which can be combined in different ways by the children themselves or by the adults setting up a particular activity in response to an observed interest.

Think about how staff at the Mandela Children's Centre have resourced their outdoor play space:

We have limited resources and decided against having a fixed climbing frame, opting instead for found, natural and open ended materials.

We have a selection of logs and tree trunks, large and small; a collection of plastic milk crates; a large sand tray and two large water trays; a woodwork bench equipped with wooden and real tools; some bikes and tries and prams and wheeled toys; a set of large wooden building blocks which are stored in the shed; wooden plants and five A frames. We have some large plastic and wooden boxes and often collect empty cardboard boxes from the local shops. We have lengths of fabric, some rubber tyres, things which can be hit hanging down from string; an empty water barrel, plastic hoops, a collection of containers, balls, bats, ropes, and so on. A parent gave us a tent which we sometimes erect and which is popular. Inside we put things like cushions and home corner equipment and torches.

Set 1: The early learning goals for movement

There are three early learning goals related to developing movement:

> Move with confidence, imagination and in safety.

> Move with control and coordination.

> Travel around, under, over and through balancing and climbing equipment.

Do you think that you have to plan for physical development or is it enough just to make sure that the climbing frame, the hoops and ropes and the balance beams are in place? If you want children to grow in confidence and to refine their skills, you need to plan for progression in physical development just as you do for other areas of learning. This means that you need to plan what you will make available in the outdoor play area each day. It is important to remember not to offer the same activities and materials day in and day out. If you do this, you remove the possibility for children to develop increasing control and awareness. Do remember the theory of 'Match' mentioned in an earlier chapter, which suggests that something should be added to or removed from a situation in order to take learning forward, but that this change should be carefully matched to the child's interests and needs.

Think about how the following examples illustrate this:

A worker at the Rainbow Playgroup noticed that four-year-old Tamina, who was very small for her age, was finding it difficult to join her friends in playing on the climbing frame because she found the height of the first step daunting. The worker placed a wooden block at the base of the steps. She observed what happened and was intrigued to find that not only did this block achieve her aim of giving Tamina the confidence to climb up the steps but that the other children used the block as something to leap over when they came down the steps.

The staff at a playgroup working in a church hall with no access to outdoor space have set up 'A' frames with planks in order to ensure the children have some opportunity every day to develop some physical skills. Using only two 'A' frames and three planks of wood, they are able to vary the layout so that children are offered 'bridges' to walk across, ramps to climb up and slide down, and enclosed areas to explore. The addition of objects like blankets, torches, picnic baskets a steering wheel and some milk crates allows the children to turn the 'A' frames into different environments to explore.

Planning for the outdoors is crucial and something that is not always done with as much care and attention as planning what is on offer indoors. Many practitioners find planning what the adults will do outdoors difficult. Sometimes this is because they become preoccupied with the role of the adults being to do with safety, and this is, of course, a consideration. But being out-side and just being 'on the lookout' is not enough.

The coordinator of Amandla Early Years Unit asked her staff to plan what aspects of physical development would be catered for each week. This involved the staff in much discussion about what physical skills the children needed to acquire or refine and what materials and resources they should offer. One planning sheet looked like that shown in Figure 6.1.

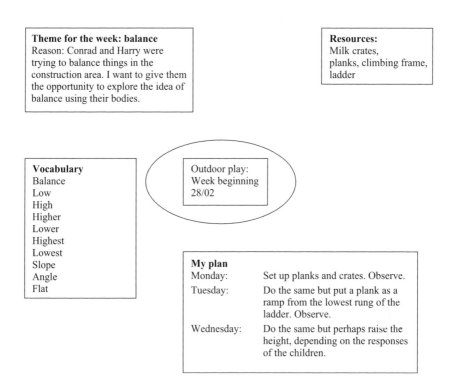

Theme for the week: balance
Reason: Conrad and Harry were trying to balance things in the construction area. I want to give them the opportunity to explore the idea of balance using their bodies.

Resources:
Milk crates,
planks, climbing frame,
ladder

Vocabulary
Balance
Low
High
Higher
Lower
Highest
Lowest
Slope
Angle
Flat

Outdoor play:
Week beginning
28/02

My plan
Monday: Set up planks and crates. Observe.
Tuesday: Do the same but put a plank as a ramp from the lowest rung of the ladder. Observe.
Wednesday: Do the same but perhaps raise the height, depending on the responses of the children.

Figure 6.1 Example of a playgroup's weekly planning sheet.

Think again about what the role of the adult is when children are busily engaged in exploring physical space. Do you think it is about ensuring that the children are safe or is there more involved?

It has already been said that many practitioners are so intent on ensuring that children are playing safely (which is, of course, essential) that they ignore the possibilities inherent in the situation for intervening appropriately and scaffolding learning.

Read through the case study below and then try to identify where you, the adult, might have intervened in order to extend learning. Try to say what you might have said or done.

Rehan, Jo, Beth and Akinola (who has very little English) are all four years old. They are out in the garden playing on the climbing frame. Rehan is 'in charge'. He is leading the other children and telling them what to do. They follow his suggestions happily until Beth, climbing up on to the plank which goes from one frame to another, loses her balance and nearly falls. She starts to cry and Jo rushes over to comfort her. Akinola, meanwhile, climbs down, goes inside and fetches a cushion from the book corner which he places underneath the plank. He urges Beth to have another go. She refuses and goes indoors. Jo starts to hang upside down from the rungs and swings to and fro, shouting 'My head's down! My head's down!' Akinola climbs down and stands beneath Jo watching her in fascination. Then he climbs up again and attempts to hang upside down.

How did you get on? There are no right or wrong answers because we are all individuals and will see things differently and interact differently. But you will have seen many points at which you might have intervened. For example, Akinola's obvious concern for Beth and his action in fetching the cushion offered the opportunity for the adult to reflect back to him the importance of his action by saying something like, 'That was such a thoughtful thing to do, Aki. You were making sure that if Beth fell she wouldn't hurt herself.' Did you also consider the many opportunities in this example for introducing some of the language of position and comparison? Notice here the links with mathematical development.

Set 2: The early learning goal related to developing a sense of space

There is only one learning goal related to developing a sense of space:

Show awareness of space, of themselves and of others.

You can see how the children in the above example are exploring space and beginning to understand their own capabilities and those of their peers. Offering opportunities for the exploration of space on a large scale almost inevitably offers children opportunities for play together. Children need to be aware of other children as they climb and jump, run and ride bikes. They need to take turns on the climbing frame and negotiate who is going to do what. And as they play with other children, they use language in a meaningful and active context. Listen to your children as they talk in their play and you will find evidence of this. Vygotsky (1978) reminds us that 'Learning awakens a variety of internal developmental processes that are able to operate only when the child is interacting with people in his environment and in co-operation with his peers.'

A final word in this section about risk-taking. The concern for children's safety often overrides everything. Many practitioners place restrictions on children which limit their opportunities to explore fully. This is not always confined to the outdoor area. Some practitioners limit the number of children who can play in the home corner or who can use the woodwork bench or who can be at the water tray. Such restrictions remove autonomy from the child and make the child dependent on the adult to define what is possible. You might like to remind yourself that one of the characteristics of play is that it allows children to take risks, because children set their own agenda.

This is an area which often gives rise to fierce argument between practitioners. Obviously you need to ensure that the environment you provide is as safe as possible, but you also need to consider whether you have made it so safe that little learning can take place. It is important to allow children to take 'safe risks'. After all, if there are five children in the home corner rather than the four you have stipulated, what is the danger? The danger is that you, the adult, are less in control. The children will regulate themselves. When the home corner becomes too crowded, play becomes difficult and the children have to resolve this situation for themselves – an excellent opportunity for problem-solving and negotiating. Similarly, when considering outdoor play, think carefully about whether you need to limit the numbers of children on the climbing frame or try to restrict what they do.

Set 3: The early learning goals which relate to children becoming aware of health and their own bodies

There are two early learning goals relating to children's becoming aware of health and their own bodies:

Recognise the importance of keeping healthy and those things which contribute to this.

Recognise the changes that happen to their bodies when they are active.

In developing countries, much more attention is paid to things like health and nutrition in terms of promoting children's learning and development. In many of these countries, issues of health and nutrition and poverty are fixed more firmly in the minds of practitioners, and it is well recognised that the physical and emotional conditions children are exposed to may impact on their learning and development. Hungry children, children who are ill, children who have suffered war or abuse are not likely to thrive. An awareness of the conditions of the children in your group is important. These early learning goals offer practitioners opportunities to think more carefully about a number of issues:

- the variety of family expectations and practices in terms of health and nutrition;
- the particular health needs of individual children, particularly those with special needs;
- involving children in understanding the importance of basic hygiene procedures;
- promoting independence; and
- helping children learn to make choices and articulate these.

Think about your own responses to each of these points and then read the comments below:

I went to teach in Southern Africa and somehow just took it for granted that all the children would know something about healthy eating. I found, in fact, that some of the parents believed that a child's diet should include a lot of carbo-hydrates and sugar, and that things like fruit and vegetables were not regarded as essential.

When I first started teaching I thought 'special needs' referred to children with some obvious and difficult problem – children in wheelchairs or with a hearing loss, for example. I later learned that children may have a special need on one day. For example, a child in my reception class came in one day very angry – throwing things around the room. I found out that her mother had been rushed into hospital and she was clearly very anxious. That seemed to me a special need.

It seems obvious to me that we should talk to children about basic hygiene and safety procedures and involve them in taking action to keep themselves safe. I am thinking about things like washing their hands after using the toilet, cleaning the table tops before having fruit or milk, washing the dolls and their clothes when we have a tidying session and so on.

Making choices seems, to me, the essence of what we want children to be able to do. We want them to be able to articulate what it is they want to do or to eat or to make or to look at and we want them to be able to follow these desires and then reflect on what it was like.

Set 4: The early learning goals for using equipment:

There are two early learning goals for using equipment:

Use a range of small and large equipment.

Handle tools, objects, construction and malleable materials safely and with increasing control.

The ability to use tools is essential to life. By tools we mean any of the huge number of objects we use as extensions of our hands in our everyday lives – things like a pen, toothbrush, pencil, broom, lawnmower, computer, and so on. Tools are an extension not only of our hands, but also of our minds. If you use a window pole to open a window, the pole serves as an extension to your body and enables you to perform something you would not be able to do without using the tool. If you use a pen to write down some ideas, the tool acts as an extension of your mind.

Tools are often specific to a culture, and all human beings belong to cultural groups. Learning to use and to make cultural tools is an essential part of being human. In the early years of life – the years described by Piaget as the Sensori-motor stage – young children spend a great deal of time exploring the objects they encounter. They move on from asking, 'What is this thing? What does it do?' to asking, 'What can I do with this? What can I use it for?' By the time children start in the playgroup or nursery they have often had a great deal of experience of exploring the objects in their world and will continue to do so, refining their skills and enhancing their learning.

It follows from this that skilled early years practitioners will pay a great deal of attention to the tools and objects they offer children and to the activities in which these tools and objects are set.

Think about how Rainbow Playgroup organises its curriculum and its space to allow for children's exploration of tools and materials. You might want to remember that in this group there are children from different cultural groups – Turkish children, Bangladeshi children, Polish children, and so on. See whether you think the cultural tools of these children are evident.

The staff set up a **graphics area** (or **writing table**) and offered the children the following tools, all in labelled containers or set out on stencils:

- pencils
- a range of felt-tipped pens
- crayons
- ballpoint pens
- rubbers (erasers)
- Tippex
- scissors (both left- and right-handed)
- a hole punch
- a stapler
- glue sticks
- sticky tape
- masking tape
- rulers
- calligraphy pens
- paintbrushes
- computer keyboard.

In the **technology** (or **workshops**) **area** the following tools are on offer:

- various kinds of glue
- assorted boxes
- cartons and containers all sorted according to size and shape
- large sheets of wrapping paper
- foil
- butterfly clips
- string
- tissue paper
- scissors
- stapler
- sticky tape
- masking tape
- paste spreaders
- elastic bands.

In the **woodwork area** are:

- a woodwork bench
- a vice
- a saw
- hammers

- nails and panel pins
- a selection of pieces of wood
- wood glue.

A variety of **malleable materials** (dough, cornflour and water, clay, etc.) are offered, with all or some of the following:

- a garlic press
- a cheese grater
- wooden rollers
- pastry cutters
- straws
- cookie tins
- knives
- spoons
- forks
- chopsticks
- objects that can be used for leaving an imprint (like Stickle bricks).

In the **construction area** are:

- a set of large Community Playthings blocks set out on stencils
- a set of small Community Playthings blocks similarly organised
- a railway set
- several construction toys like Lego, Duplo, Mobilo, etc.
- vehicles
- two wooden planks to act as ramps
- some shiny strips of linoleum
- some rough strips of cardboard.

In the **home corner** are:

- cups and saucers
- a teapot
- a Turkish coffee pot
- bowls
- chopsticks
- a wok
- knives and forks
- spoons of different sizes
- slotted spoons
- ladles
- a spaghetti spoon.

In their planning notes the staff plan that some of these activities will be set up outdoors each day, offering children the opportunity to develop their fine motor skills both indoors and out.

Do you feel that resources like this would be equally appropriate in reception classes?

Clearly, a good deal of thought has gone into planning the resources described above. Some of them are costly (like a woodwork bench and the Community Playthings blocks) but most are not and can easily be gathered together and maintained. It is important that resources are set out in such a way that children can follow their own plans through and find the resources they need without having to call on an adult. Of course, adults do need to be on hand in order to interact, to help, to demonstrate sometimes, to observe what the children are doing and to scaffold learning.

The difficult question of safety arises again. Some practitioners are reluctant to let children use woodwork tools or to use things like a garlic press. Often children are offered scissors which are so blunt that they will not cut. If children are to explore tools and to get involved in the processes they have determined for themselves, it is essential that they are offered tools that work and that are cared for. Of course there are dangers, but children are generally sensible and respond well to being given some autonomy. Practitioners need to show children how to use the tools and explain to them that a saw, for example, is sharp and has to be used with care. They also need to involve the children in caring for the resources so that the next time they want to use them they are still in working order.

You may be interested in two examples of children exploring tools which were observed in a nursery in Reggio Emilia:

A table had been set out for the children with rulers, sticky tape, long strips of paper, glue, shiny objects, pieces of cardboard, pairs of scissors and pencils. The children were free to use the materials in any way they chose. Some children spent more than two hours at the table, rolling up strips of paper and gluing them on to other surfaces.

At the clay table a group of children were working with an adult trying to make human figures out of clay. The children were aged between four and six. The adult offered them some simple stands made of two pieces of wood at right angles to each other. This formed a sort of support around which the clay figure could be constructed. When the adult was asked what had prompted her to come up with this brilliant device, she said that she had noticed that the children had difficulty in constructing three-dimensional figures out of clay because the legs were often too thin to support the body. As a result, the figures made by the children were often two-dimensional and the children quickly lost interest in making these, since their intention had been to make three-dimensional figures.

Summary
- You will all already offer children many opportunities to explore the physical world. The important points to remember are that children need access to as many experiences as possible in order that their learning continues – in other words, in order that they are able to gain increasing control of both their fine and their gross motor skills. You will want to consider how you can offer a safe and stimulating environment which allows children to take 'safe' risks.
- Children, from a very early age, explore the physical world through movement and through the exploration of the objects they encounter.
- Physical development has consequences for all aspects of development – cognitive, linguistic, social and emotional.
- Practitioners need to ensure that children are able to develop and refine their existing skills through a carefully planned programme and thoughtful resourcing.
- The role of the adult is more than a supervisory one. As in all areas of learning, adults need to observe, to scaffold learning, to interact, to demonstrate, to explain, to listen, to offer help and to support in as many ways as possible.
- Although it is essential to ensure that children play and learn in a safe environment, thought needs to be given to allowing children to take risks in order to become autonomous.
- Practitioners will want to pay attention to the range of tools and materials they offer to children.
- Collaborative play is easily fostered through physical play, particularly outdoors.
- Practitioners will want to explain to children how to use tools safely.
- Practitioners will want to involve children in caring for the equipment in their nursery or playgroup.
- Tools and equipment that are not properly cared for insult the child and limit the children's abilities to accomplish the purposes they have set in their play.

Chapter 7

Exploring the world and expressing ideas

We have looked at how children seek to understand the world and the objects in it. They also seek to understand and explain wider aspects of the world. They ask questions about how things happen and why: they want to know how things used to be; they want to know what it is like in places they encounter in books, on television or through family links. And through their explorations they attempt to express their ideas and thoughts and feelings as they represent what they learn. In the Foundation Stage, two areas of learning are involved: 'knowledge and understanding of the world' and 'creative development'.

In terms of coming to develop the skills, knowledge and understanding to help them make sense of the world, children need activities based, as always, on first-hand experiences that will encourage them to observe, question, make guesses, try things out, solve problems, make predictions, identify patterns, think critically and discuss. This means that practitioners need to set up challenging activities inside and out, activities which are imaginative and enjoyable and open-ended. Adults need to consider how they can help the children express their ideas and to assess children's progress, as they do in all other learning areas.

Knowledge and understanding of the world

Knowledge and understanding of the world is a broad area of learning which encompasses the means by which children come to understand the world in which they live. What children explore and learn in this area lays the foundations for later work in science, design and technology, history, geography, and information and communication technology (ICT). Through practical, first-hand activities children should have opportunities to think about where they live, how things are now, how things used to be, how things are made, what things are made of, why things happen, how things change, and so on. In their explorations and investigations they need many opportunities to use a range of tools: computers, magnifiers, gardening or woodworking tools, screwdrivers, pens and paintbrushes, for example. They also need opportunities to work with a range of materials and with materials that may change their form – for example, wet and dry sand, coloured and clear liquids, thin glue and thick glue, fine pens and thick pens. To begin to understand the past in ways that are meaningful they might need opportunities to explore everyday artefacts and see how they have changed. These could include toys or vehicles or machines for playing music. As in all work with young children, the artefacts they explore and consider should be those that are familiar to children in order for them to be able to draw on their prior experience.

Set 1: The early learning goals for exploration and investigation

There are four early learning goals for exploration and investigation:

Investigate objects and materials by using all of their senses as appropriate.

Find out about and identify some features of living things, objects and events they observe.

Look closely at similarities, differences, patterns and change.

Ask questions about why things happen and how things work.

These learning goals relate primarily to utilising children's curiosity about their world to enable them to develop a range of skills for investigating what they see and what interests them. This is what can be called the 'scientific process'. Anyone who encounters something new, unfamiliar and interesting struggles to understand it. Young children want to know all sorts of things like why hair grows and grows, how babies are made, why things with wheels roll, why things that are dropped always fall to the ground. In order for them to ask these questions they have to have gone through this scientific process. Let us take the example of the child wondering why things that are dropped always fall to the ground and examine the processes involved.

Basically, what happens is that the child observes something which raises a question in his or her mind. The child notices that an object, when dropped, always falls to the ground. So, the child decides to see whether this applies only to some objects or to all objects. The child spends hours (maybe even days) dropping large and small objects. In doing this the child is testing out his or her hypothesis. At some point the child realises that all objects, when dropped, will fall to the ground. In other words, the child has arrived at some sort of conclusion. This process – observing, questioning, hypothesising, testing and concluding – is what scientists do as they try to uncover some of the laws and patterns of the physical and natural worlds. Susan Isaacs ran a school in the 1920s which was structured around the principle that young children should be offered a rich and stimulating environment in which they would encounter problems to excite their imaginations and invite them to find solutions. The staff at the Malting House School were all trained to observe children closely and to let children follow their own interests.

Susan Isaacs herself wrote a fascinating book (called *Intellectual Growth in Young Children* and now sadly out of print) in which she records some of the observations and gives dramatic evidence of children learning and developing through their own explorations and the responses of the adults. One of her most fascinating examples concerns the death of one of the rabbits at the school.

When the children came in one morning and found the rabbit lying in its hutch they discussed whether or not it was dead. Then one of the children said he knew how to find out. He said they needed to put the rabbit in water to see if it floated. His hypothesis was that dead things sink and living things float. The children put the rabbit in the water and noticed that it moved in the water. They concluded that the rabbit was still alive. Now Susan Isaacs, working with these children, helped them make the next step in learning and understanding. She brought the children a twig, which all the children agreed was not alive. The children put the twig in the water and it, too, was moved by the currents in the water. The children were able to realise that it was the current which had moved the rabbit and that the rabbit was, indeed, dead. What happened next arouses strong feelings in some readers. The children buried the rabbit, but a few days later started to hypothesise about whether the rabbit was still underground or if it had gone 'to heaven'. Susan Isaacs allowed the children to dig up the dead rabbit, which they examined with great interest and a huge amount of passionate discussion.

The children in your setting will be behaving like little scientists in many situations. To stimulate their curiosity and learning you might like to consider what situations and resources will best enhance this learning.

Think about Rainbow Playgroup's approach to exploration and investigation. Does it seem to you to offer appropriate resources and is this enough?

At the Rainbow Playgroup staff have paid attention to the resources they can gather together to offer opportunities for children to behave scientifically. The resources include things like batteries, bulbs, magnets, mirrors, motors and gears, pumps and torches, screwdrivers, sieves and tubes. They have gathered together collections of things – things that roll, things that reflect, things that stretch, things that are transparent. They ensure there is a good range of natural objects, living things, found objects, and to help children refine their skills of observation they supply midispectors and magnifying glasses.

To help children explore sound they offer things to bang, to pluck, to vibrate, to scratch and to shake.

You will agree, I am sure, that this is a good starting point for enabling children to find the tools they need to aid their explorations and investigations.

Think about the role of adults in the examples below.

Staff in one of the nursery classes at Amandla Early Years Unit noticed that children's play in the sand had become rather repetitive. They set out the sand in two small containers – one with wet sand and one with dry. On the table next to the trays they placed some miniature scoops, some tea-strainers, some shiny objects, some cut-up straws and some small moulds. The adults here had been attentive to what the children were doing and had changed one activity slightly in order to move them on in their learning.

When the weather turned very cold, the teacher in a reception class asked the children whether they would like to do an experiment. She asked them to suggest what they could do to find out how ice is made. Following the children's suggestions and allowing them to select containers, a range of dishes and bowls were filled with water, fruit juice and milk. Some containers were put outdoors; the others left indoors. 'All of these are liquid, aren't they,' asked the teacher. 'Yes,' said Luigi. 'We can drink them all.' 'Shall we put out something that's solid, do you think?' asked the teacher. There followed a long discussion about what else to set out and the final result included a bowl of yoghurt (which the children said was not liquid and not solid!), a bowl of breakfast cereal and a bowl of cut-up apple. The teacher then led the children in predicting what would happen to each bowl. She recorded their predictions. The next morning the children rushed in to test out their hypotheses. The teacher, who had no scientific training herself, managed to use words to extend the vocabularies of the children – words like 'freeze', 'predict', 'ice', 'liquid', 'solid'. She also helped them become aware of what it was that they were doing as they made guesses, constructed a test, carried it out and arrived at some conclusions.

Set 2: The early learning goals for designing and making skills

There are two early learning goals for designing and making skills:

Build and construct with a wide range of objects, selecting appropriate resources, and adapting their work where necessary.

Select the tools and techniques they need to shape, assemble and join the materials they are using.

You will know how much children enjoy making or building things. A child will happily spend a very long time making something totally unrecognisable to the adult eye but deeply satisfying to the child. The researchers Gunther Kress and Kate Pahl have done a lot of very interesting research into exactly what happens when children engage in this work. The process involves planning what to make, choosing the materials and tools for the task, making the environment or object, reviewing it and making changes where necessary.

Think about what you learn from the following two examples:

Donna is constructing in the brick area. She is trying to make a bridge. She gathers together some cylindrical blocks and places them in a line with spaces between them. She then gets a plank of wood to lay across the top of them. The plank she has chosen is too short to cover all the cylinders. She stops, looks carefully, tries the plank two or three more times and then carefully removes two cylinders. This time the plank fits.

In the reception class all the children are being asked to make a card for Mother's Day. They have all been given a piece of card and some pictures they can cut out of magazines. They then copy the message from the board.

It should be obvious that in the first example the child is actively learning, actively exploring and investigating and using what she finds in order to create something of her own choosing. She is playing. She finds the resources, tries out her plan, stops to evaluate, makes some decision, carries that out and completes her project. In the second example – and one that is still very common in classes across the country – the children are following a recipe given them by the adults. What they are making is not of their choosing and very culture specific. They cannot choose the resources. They do not even attempt to write their own message.

Children are only likely to get deeply involved in their construction and making where they can make choices and find what they need. Here is how Rainbow Playgroup set up a 'workshop area':

We ask parents to bring in materials for this on a regular basis. At first all the empty cartons and boxes were just dumped into a large container, but we discovered that the children were just taking the thing at the top and not making proper choices. So we rearranged this and managed to get the parents to put their offerings in the correct container. We have several large plastic containers and they are labelled. All the toilet rolls and long cylinders go in one: circles (lids and things like that) in another; large boxes, small boxes, tubs, and so on. Then we have made stencils of the shapes of the objects and put the objects on them: a stapler, Sellotape, masking tape, pairs of scissors, rulers and so on. We mix glue every morning and children know that they can go and get the woodwork glue from the work bench if they need it.

As well as all this we collect attractive things and store these in labelled containers – things like sequins, beads, bits of fabric, cut up wrapping paper, pictures, small objects the children bring in, feathers, ribbon, and so on. Then we also provide lots and lots of different sizes and shapes of paper. We have rolls of foil, sheets of wrapping paper, sheets of shiny paper and sheets of tissue paper. We explain to the children that these are expensive and should be used with care. We were amazed at how responsive the children were. Sometimes we hear them saying things like 'I'm going to use some of that 'spensive shiny stuff 'cos this is for my mummy!'

The technology area was the first area of our room we paid attention to and it remains very popular with the children. We often timetable an adult to be there, but even when no adult is actually based there we set it up in the mornings with something slightly different each day. The children spend a very long time in there, getting deeply involved in what they are making. We have noticed that it is an area where there is a lot of talk going on and are aware of the fact that, since it is not dependent on children being able to speak English, all the children in the room use it.

And here is how some children playing at home made things to follow their own interest. The point of including this is to illustrate that learning is never dependent on expensive resourcing.

Hannah and Ben brought some string round to the house of their grandmother because they had started a game which involved making a set of small doll's-house toys slide down ropes, parachute off the staircase, cope with broken limbs, and so on. They used masking tape, discarded paper plates and cups, bits of toothpick, onion skins and other found objects to create an elaborate and complex scenario which continued over several visits and brought together design and making, science and story. One of the dolls fell and was then said to have broken his leg. This involved a quick trip to the hospital in the kitchen and the putting on of a plaster cast (made of onion skin) and the creation of a crutch, made of toothpicks.

Set 3: The early learning goals for information and communication technology

There is one early learning goal for ICT:

> **Find out about and identify the uses of everyday technology and use information and communication technology and programmable toys to support their learning.**

Many settings have no access to computers and many offer the computer as 'an activity', not necessarily thinking about how to use it as a tool for children to use to support their learning. There are now many programs produced particularly for young children, but if you use these you need to examine them and consider just how they support learning. Young children will enjoy just playing with the keyboard and watching what happens on the screen when they press keys. This physical exploration is an essential stage of learning, and children who do this are not 'messing about'. Adults can certainly interact with children as they explore the effects of their actions, explaining the purpose of keys and symbols. Older children may attempt to find particular significant letters on the keyboard – perhaps those to be found in their names. The symbols on the keyboard are, of course, upper-case letters; you may want to buy or make a template of lower-case letters to fit over the keys.

There are some interesting things for children to do on computers, one of which involves them designing things that move. This requires a great deal of what might be called 'possibility thinking' – i.e. raising questions like 'What would happen if . . . ?' This type of thinking is one that is closely linked not only to exploring and explaining the world but also to representing the world – which is what we will look at in the next section.

Young children will also enjoy the effects of using one of the many paint programs available, particularly if you have access to a colour screen and colour printer.

There are a number of programmable toys and you may find that children are familiar with them and adept at using them. Here is an example from the reception class:

The class has two Roamers and the children play with them frequently. One of the nursery nurses decided to link this activity with a story she had been reading to the children. She brought in some props – a plastic castle, some plastic dinosaurs, a small doll and some other toys – and then made up a story about how the prince in the Roamer had to rescue the princess in the castle and to do so had to navigate round some obstacles. The children were deeply involved and totally engrossed, and found programming the Roamer a meaningful thing that they could sometimes manage unaided.

Do remember to routinely use tape recorders and cameras, particularly digital cameras, in your work with young children. These are wonderful for recording children's work in order to make books, to put in children's files or to send home.

Set 4: The early learning goals for a sense of time

There is one early learning goal for a sense of time:

Find out about past and present events in their own lives and those of their families and other people they know.

For young children, living primarily in the here and now, concepts about time are difficult and there is little to be achieved by introducing topics such as 'A Victorian Classroom'. A child in a London school recently told his family that for their class assembly they were 'doing' 'Henry the Eighth and teeth', and five-year-old Andy, in a reception class in Manchester, amused everyone by bringing home her project book about 'Nelson'. On one page was a picture she had drawn and on the next the writing: 'Here is Nelson wearing his best dress for cleaning the deck.' You can see how meaningless topics like that are for young children. But young children are interested in their own lives and the lives of people close to them, and some interesting things can be done around these themes to meet this early learning goal. So, bringing in the clothes their parents wore when they were young, or reading stories about 'long ago', are ways of helping children think about the past and the present and sometimes the future.

Set 5: The early learning goals for a sense of place

There are two early learning goals in relation to a sense of place:

Observe, find out about, and identify features in the place they live and the natural world.

Find out about their environment and talk about those features they like and dislike.

Lettie, one of the practitioners in the playgroup, has brought in a photograph of herself as a baby. She has also collected some baby things for the children to explore. She is hoping that the children will start talking about the new baby at home or about when they were babies. She plans to ask parents to bring in photographs of their own children as babies and has invited Dario's mother to bring her new baby in to show the children. She also plans to set up a baby clinic in a corner of the room. The children arrive and all cluster round her, picking up the bibs and bottles and baby clothes, and are very intrigued by the photograph.

'Look,' shouts Sam in glee, 'no hair.'

'I didn't have hair when I was a baby,' responds Lettie, 'but then it grew and now I have got long hair, haven't I?'

'My baby got hair,' contributes Filiz, who very rarely says anything since she is in the early stages of acquiring English.

What can you do to help children develop their ideas and knowledge about their own world?

Many playgroups, nursery classes and reception classes build outings into their programme. These can range from outings to the local shops in order to buy the materials for cooking or outings to the local park or to travel on local transport. Visits such as these allow children to make the links between home and nursery and to build on their prior experience. Older children will enjoy visits to places of interest – perhaps to a building site or to a museum or to see a place of particular local interest. You would obviously link the visit to the children's interests and the ongoing work of the nursery group. In doing this you will think about what you can do, before the visit, to prepare the children to get the most out of it. You will also consider what to do within your setting after the visit in order to allow children to build on the experience.

Think about what you can learn from these examples:

We took the children to the fire station and I took along a camera. When we got back, the children all wanted to draw pictures and we agreed that we would make a Big Book about the visit. We used both photographs and children's drawings, and the children, with my help, constructed the text, which I wrote up in big print in front of them. This gave them a model of how writing works. I also made sure that I had got together some resources for them to use in their imaginative play: some plastic helmets, two small ladders and lots of lengths of hosepipe.

We took the children to the local market where there is a stall that sells seeds. When we got back we set up a plant stall and the children all planted their seeds and labelled them (using invented writing or copying the letters on the seed packets). We talked about how plants need water, and the children were really reliable about looking after their plants. They put prices on them and got out the till and the plastic money. One child got some wrapping paper from the technology area to wrap up the plants she was selling. The next day a parent brought in armfuls of cut flowers which the children could also sell at the stall. It was a great success.

Next to the school there is a lot of building going on. I arranged with the site manager to take a group of children across. The children were fascinated with what was going on. When we got back we set up a section of the garden as a construction site. I got together some pairs of Wellington boots, some shovels and forks and some safety helmets. The children carried over planks of wood and large wooden blocks. Two children set up a 'site office' and asked me for some clipboards. The play went on for weeks and involved a great deal of talk and a lot of writing. It was brilliant.

In addition to planning outings and their follow-up, you will want to ensure that you have some books which will extend children's learning about their world. There are many excellent information books available for young children. If you do not already own these in your setting and if funds are limited, you can borrow them from the library. So, if you have set up a baby clinic, you might want to borrow books about babies; if you have set up a garage, you might want books about cars and vehicles. And do remember that things like DIY manuals, placed in your imaginative play areas, will spark off a great deal of talk and exploration.

At this point it is important to remind ourselves of a principle of early learning: young children need to be able to see the significance of what they are doing. In other words, they need to make the links between their lives and their experience and what is offered to them. History, for young children, is very brief – perhaps only as long as their own lives. Similarly, young children will want to explore their immediate and slightly wider environment, and where you have children in your group who have been born in other countries or who have travelled abroad, setting up an aeroplane or turning your home corner into a non-traditional non-English home may be very effective. The key is to link what you offer to the children's experience so that they can build on this. This brings us back to the essential tenet of good early years practice – that it builds on individual children's needs, experience and interests and allows children, in situations that make human sense to them, to learn through play and with the sensitive support of adults. Visits will also help children discover the purposes of some of the features they notice in their environment. Young children, starting in your setting, will already have discovered that shops are there to sell things, that banks are there for people to get money from, that bus stops are where people wait when they want to take a bus. You can build on this knowledge by reproducing some of these features within your setting. Some playgroups have noticed how play is sustained when they have set up things like a post office, a garage, a bus station, a restaurant or a supermarket within the setting.

Set 6: The early learning goals for culture and beliefs

There is one early learning goal in connection with culture and beliefs:

> **Begin to know about their own cultures and beliefs and those of other people.**

This is a key early learning goal. We are all situated in a culture (or cultures) and a community. Within our culture are the things that define us as both unique and part of a group. Our culture defines the words we use, the values and beliefs we hold, the ways in which we relate to our parents or our children or older people. And we all – even those of us in, say, deepest

Suffolk – live in a world rich in diversity. We all see people who are different from us in the streets or on television. We all eat foods and listen to music that come from across the world. One of the key things early childhood practitioners can do is to enable children to learn to live easily in this richly diverse world – free of stereotypes, prejudice or discrimination. Thinking about the different languages, beliefs, customs and traditions of others is part of this, but it is important that this is not done in a tokenist way, with a colourful celebration of 'festivals' seen as being enough. This goals is about much more than that, and you will see the links between this and some of the goals for personal, social and emotional development.

Here are some incidents recorded in nursery classes, playgroups and reception classes across the country. They are all real examples. Which do you think will enable children to learn to celebrate their own cultures and develop respect for those of others?

The class has an assembly for Mother's Day and all the children sing a song in assembly about 'Mummy does the cooking' and 'Mummy does the washing'.

The project in the reception class is 'bread' and each week a different type of bread is baked, often with the help of parents and family or community members.

There is a collection of musical instruments from around the world that children have constant – and noisy – access to.

Andy comes home from school and demands to be christened because everyone else in her reception class has been.

Summary
- Knowledge and understanding of the world encompasses a very wide area of learning and development. Providing for this learning is a vital part of the role of all practitioners, and one of the best ways of doing this is to remember that children learn best where they are able to see the point of what they are doing and where they are able to build on what they already know.
- As young children strive to understand their world, they want to know about how and why things happen; about people and their relationships; about their own lives and families both now and in the 'touchable' past.

continued on next page

- Practitioners will want to help children find answers to the questions they raise by setting up meaningful contexts within the setting, using appropriate information books and taking children on visits and outings into the local community.
- Practitioners will show an interest in children's developing ideas and concepts and will encourage children to talk about these in context rather than in testing situations. They will also provide materials for the children to use to record their ideas should they wish to do so.
- Practitioners will want to ensure that they provide many opportunities and resources for children to behave like little scientists.
- They will also offer an environment which supports children making choices in terms of materials and resources.
- Access to technology should be part of everyday activities.
- Practitioners need to remain alert to ensuring equality of access and opportunity within all the activities on offer.
- Care should be taken to ensure that what is talked about, represented and offered allows all children to learn more about their own and others' cultures, beliefs and languages.

Creative development

You will remember that Loris Malaguzzi talked of 'the hundred languages of children', by which he meant the many ways in which children can express their ideas and thoughts and findings (see p. 48). Young children need to be able to explore the world and express their findings in as many different ways as possible. This representation and re-representation of their ideas is an essential ingredient in learning.

In our society – and particularly in our schooling – we tend to place a far greater emphasis on the skills of reading, writing and numeracy than we do on the creative areas of music, dance and art, for example. Yet if you consider what enriches your life, you will probably include things like listening to music, looking at pictures, going to the cinema or theatre, or dancing. The music you enjoy and the films that please you may be different from those that please your best friend – but one of the things that makes us human is that we are moved by the ways in which other people are able to express their thoughts and ideas and feelings using whatever means they choose. You may also have come across the work of Howard Gardner, who talks of multiple intelligences. He says that we all learn differently and that our schooling system should allow for this. Our schooling system focuses primarily on reading and writing and counting, but there are many children who learn best through physical exploration and others who learn best through dance or drama. Young children who are fortunate enough to grow up in a society which values creative expression are exposed from an early age to things of beauty. The children visiting the cathedral in Modena, cited in an earlier chapter, were able not only to look at beautiful things but to have a go for themselves at expressing their ideas through drawing, painting, mime, dance, imaginative play, music and three-dimensional work. Each attempt at redescribing or re-representing ideas refined the children's concepts.

It is important to remind ourselves at this point of the importance of what Malaguzzi describes as 'the journey' that children take as they attempt to represent their ideas and feelings. This, the process, is what determines the quality of the learning. The better the journey, the deeper the learning. This applies to children making marks on paper, constructing three-dimensional objects or structures, moving in response to music, or any other situation in which children become deeply engaged in expressing their ideas, thoughts and feelings.

Let us now look in detail at the early learning goals for this learning area:

Set 1: The early learning goals for exploring media and materials

There is one early learning goal for exploring media and materials:

> **Explore colour, texture, shape, form and space in two and three dimensions.**

In considering the opportunities you already provide for children to explore their world and the objects in it, you will become aware that this particular learning goal refers not only to creativity, but also to exploration and science, mathematics and physical development. Young children, being inherently curious, explore everything they encounter. In doing so they inevitably pay attention to how things are similar and how things are different. A child presented with three balls, two of which are blue and one green, will perhaps pay attention to colour. The child offered three balls, one rubber, one wool and one plastic, may pay attention to texture. This goal offers a good example of just how difficult it is to describe young children's learning in terms of subject areas or areas of learning.

It follows from this that children need to be in an environment in which there are interesting things to explore. This does not mean that children need to have access to expensive equipment. In the developing world, children explore the natural, the made and the found objects in their environments and use these in ingenious ways to create something new. In the Italian nursery schools described earlier, staff collect 'beautiful' things for the children to touch, to examine and to explore. Together with these they offer a range of magnifying glasses and materials for painting, drawing and three-dimensional work.

You may want to think about how you can give children the experience of seeing paintings or sculpture or artefacts. One way to do this is to take children on outings to interesting places. Some nurseries take small groups of children to art galleries and museums. Many offer very appropriate programmes for young children. Another way is to get together a collection of posters, books or postcards. A third way is to invite parents to bring in objects that they find interesting or beautiful and to share these with the children. In one nursery school a teacher collected various artefacts from her holiday and brought these in for the children to touch and look at. They were simple things like shells, a length of batik fabric, a small doll, a local musical instrument.

Set 2: The early learning goals for music

There is just one early learning goal for music:

> **Recognise and explore how sounds can be changed, sing simple songs from memory, recognise repeated sounds and sound patterns and match movements to music.**

The place of music in the curriculum is an interesting one. In the BBC's series of Reith Lectures in 2006 the musician Daniel Barenboim talked about how much more emphasis is placed on looking than on listening and reminded listeners that children who have opportunities to make music, particularly to make music with other people, are able to engage in cooperative work, in negotiation, in making decisions, in expressing their feelings and in communicating widely. A question you need to ask is whether the children in your setting have opportunities to make and listen and respond to music. Young children hear music all around them and many children respond to music by singing, moving to the music, using parts of their body to emphasise the rhythms. Do try to ensure that your children are invited to listen to many different types of music. It is easy nowadays to get hold of tapes of music from all over the world and you might want to think about putting a tape recorder with a selection of taped music in the home corner. Some practitioners still have a 'ring time', and in one setting this was often used as the time to introduce a tiny snatch of classical music to the children. Whilst the children were passing round their morning fruit, the teacher put on a brief excerpt of music and talked to the children about it. Even the youngest children were responsive.

You will want to encourage various things in providing opportunities for children to explore music. First, you will want to help children, through listening to music, to respond in a personal and creative way. Thus, you will want

to offer children opportunities to listen to a range of music and respond to their reaction to the music in a way which focuses on what the child is paying attention to. You may comment on the fact that the child is clapping in time to the music, or that the child has noticed that the music is fast, or that the child says that the music makes him or her feel sad.

You will want to offer children opportunities to make music for themselves. You will ensure that singing songs is an integral part of your curriculum and that you include variety in your songs so as to reflect the languages and cultures of the children. You will want children also to have access to a range of things to pluck, bang, scrape, blow, shake and vibrate. There are many very attractive musical instruments available nowadays, and many of these will be familiar to children from their own homes and communities. It is important that children have ongoing access to these instruments. It is only through their own explorations of the instruments that they will discover what the instruments do and what the effects of their own body movements will have on the instruments. You may want to offer children opportunities to make their own musical instruments and to have a go at 'writing' music just as they 'write' stories. In order to do this you would make sure that children can find examples of written music (song books provide an excellent example) and that they have manuscript paper on which to write.

Think about these examples of how some settings make music an integral part of their curriculum:

We went on a course where we learned some musical games to play with the children. So at story time we often incorporate these games in our session. One of them involves singing a song around the group about the children's names. We sing 'My name is Annie. What is your name?' and the child sings back, 'My name is Nikiwe. What is your name?' and points to another child. Then we sometimes give the children instruments and ask them to follow the 'conductor', who uses her hands to signal loud and soft: raising the hand means loud, lowering it means soft. On one occasion we asked the children to find anything in the room that would make a sound (and we had removed the instruments). They were amazing. They brought spoons to bang together, elastic bands to vibrate, blocks to knock against each other, corrugated card to strike, paper to crinkle. And sometimes we tell them to watch the conductor and to join in when the conductor points to them. Then sometimes we start off with a rhythm, just using body parts, and ask them to join in.

We now have a music corner and have in there our tape recorder and a selection of tapes. We have a range of musical instruments (bought out of the proceeds of our last jumble sale). We have made a 'music collage'. This is a large piece of card on which we have stuck things that will make a sound. We have a piece of corrugated card with a lollipop stick hanging next to it on a piece

of string; milk-bottle tops which jangle against each other; and a range of other things to bang, pluck, scrape and rattle.

We used the song 'Ten Green Bottles' as the starting point for a series of activities. The children all know the song and we often act it out. Then we made a Big Book of it and the children drew the pictures. Then we got ten green bottles and filled them with different amounts of water and set them out (making sure they were in a safe place), together with some beaters. The children were fascinated by how they could 'make tunes' by playing the bottles.

Do you have opportunities for children to respond to music by moving to it? Young children enjoy moving to music indoors and out, and this provides many opportunities for talking about the ways in which they move, the ways in which they accompany music (pluck, scrape, hit, beat, blow) and the feelings music gives rise to (sad, happy, angry, calm). The exploration of space, using their bodies, is an essential part of early learning for most children. Where children have music to listen and respond to and are encouraged to move – in any way they choose – to the sounds they hear, they use movement as a way of expressing their own ideas and feelings. Some practitioners believe that any movement or dance session needs to be highly structured. You will have to make your own decision about this.

Think about these contrasting examples to see what you feel about how to introduce opportunities for young children to move to music.

All the children have taken off their shoes and socks for a 'dance' session. The adult gets them all sitting quietly on the floor and tells them she is going to play them some music and she wants them to listen to the music and move 'quietly'. She also reminds them that when she claps her hands they must all stop and sit down. She takes the children through a series of movements – moving slowly and quickly, moving high up and low down, tiptoeing and stamping. She often models the movements for the children.

The practitioner invites any children who want to come and dance to join her in the small room. The children take off their socks and shoes. Music is already playing when they come in and the children join in enthusiastically, each moving in their own way to the movement. The adult moves among the children, commenting on what they do: 'Marko, what a huge leap you made' and 'I love the way you are twisting your arms to the music.' When the short excerpt comes to an end she invites the children to suggest what sort of music they want next. One suggests 'loud'; another shouts out 'Bob Marley' and a third says 'songs'. A decision is reached and the children, again, move to the music. Finally, the worker tells the children she has brought in some new music – something she really likes and that reminds her of when she was a little girl

and used to go to the seaside with her grandparents. She plays the tape and the children listen, some clapping, some joining in the song.

We spent a lot of money on percussion instruments and ensured that these came from Africa, from the West Indies, from America and from Europe. These are always available and children are often to be seen shaking and plucking and beating them, sometimes alone and often in groups. Children often use a chosen instrument as a model for making one of their own out of junk materials, and there is a lot of talk about this.

Set 3: The early learning goals for imagination

There is just one early learning goal for imagination:

> Use their imagination in art and design, music, dance and imaginative and role play and stories.

Perhaps, like me, you feel that this is one of the most significant of all the early learning goals. When we think about how much passion children put into their drawings and paintings, their making of models, their constructions, their making up of stories, their role-play and fantasy play it seems obvious that children have been impelled to express their ideas and feelings and use their imagination in all the ways they are offered. We want children not only to respond to the creations of others, but to have as many opportunities as possible to be creative themselves – that is, to express their own thoughts and feelings in any way they choose. We are back to the 'hundred languages of children'.

You will want to ensure that, in your setting, children are able to express their personal feelings through art (painting, drawing, collage, using clay, making things), through music (singing, playing musical instruments and making up their own musical patterns), through movement (responding to sounds and music, using gesture and mime and dancing) and through story and role-play (responding to stories, creating their own stories and acting out stories in their imaginative play).

Because there is a separate early learning goal for music, I have already addressed that. Here I will take the remaining areas in turn and suggest what materials and activities might promote children's learning.

Art

John Matthews (1994) examines young children's drawing and painting and shows, in his book *Helping Children to Draw and Paint in Early Childhood*, how these expressive acts can play a central role in the development of cognition or understanding and in the development of feelings. Matthews looked at

his own children's development and paid close attention to exactly what it was the children were attempting to describe or express. He noticed that the children's involvement in their painting and drawing was deepened where the adult concerned was able really to tune into whatever it was the child was paying attention to. Matthews reminds us that not all paintings or drawings are representational. They may not aim to represent something, but may simply reflect the child's absorption in the effects of his or her own movement, or the effect of mixing colours or what happens when two shapes are placed close together. This is an important point and one that many adults find difficult to grasp. We are so used to considering paintings as being 'of something' that we focus almost entirely on the end product.

Think carefully about what this example might teach us about how the involvement of the adult can affect the involvement of the child.

Four-year-old Martin was drawing in the playgroup. The adult came over and asked him what he had drawn. He ignored her, folded up his piece of paper and went outside to play.

The next day an adult was seated in the painting area of the playgroup observing two children. Martin came over and asked what she was doing. She explained that she was watching what the children were doing because she was interested in them. Martin put on an apron and proceeded to paint a thick red line around the edges of the paper. He then chose yellow and made some yellow dabs in the centre of his 'frame'.
    'I like those dabs you are doing, Martin,' commented the adult.
    'Yeah,' said Martin, picking up the brush in the green paint, 'and now I'm doing green dabs – dab, dab, dab.'
    He stood back to observe his painting. Then he carefully selected the red brush again and started to paint a series of vertical lines.
    'These are lines,' he announced.
    'You have done a red frame and now you are doing red lines,' commented the adult.
    'And then I am going to do some red dabs,' he said.

You will have noticed how the adult, by commenting on what Martin was doing, was able to maintain his interest and let him make choices and decisions. In this way, the language the adult used scaffolded Martin's learning and allowed him to be able to reflect on what he was doing. His interest in the activity was sustained through the adult attention. By contrast, when the adult questioned Martin about what his picture was of, he lost interest and left the drawing area. Do try to respond to a child's painting or drawing or model-making by endeavouring to focus on what it is the child seems to

be doing or paying attention to (the process), rather than expecting the child to produce something recognisable – a product.

You will want to ensure that you offer children high-quality materials that are properly cared for and you will want to involve children in caring for these materials. Here is a list of what you might want to provide:

- various different surfaces to paint on (sometimes easels, sometimes on the floor or table: paint behaves differently on an easel as compared with on a horizontal surface);
- a range of types of paper (paint, crayons and pens produce different effects on absorbent paper, shiny paper, cartridge paper, etc.);
- felt-tipped pens of different thickness; pencils; drawing pencils; water colour; poster paint; finger paint; acrylic paint; charcoal (each requires a different technique and produces a different effect);
- thick and thin paint brushes; paint rollers;
- clay and tools for using with clay;
- materials for making things.

Stories and imaginative play

You may have come across the work of Vivien Paley, who used storytelling as the main means of learning in her classroom. She encouraged the children to make up their own stories in order to make sense of their lives, and her books (which are fascinating and easy to read) show just how powerful storytelling is in terms of learning and reflection. Paley, through a long personal struggle, discovered that offering children opportunities to construct and act out stories allowed them to confront many issues in their lives and sort out their responses to these. She also discovered that observing children who were acting out through play, gave her a window into their development. You may also be interested to read the work of Ann Haas Dyson (1997) also around the power of story-making and story-enacting.

You will already offer children many opportunities to make up stories as they play in the home corner or other areas in your room. Try to ensure that the props you offer help to take children's storying and their learning forward. Younger children, more concerned with re-enacting domestic roles, will need access to 'real' things to help their play, but older children can use lengths of fabric, strips of hosepipe, empty containers – anything, in fact – to become whatever they desire.

Please remember that it is important for you, as practitioners, to take careful note of what children are doing so that activities can be provided to help them refine their skills and increase their range of experiences. Each representation and re-representation contributes to learning, and the more the opportunities for expressing feelings and thoughts, and the more sensitive the intervention of the adult, the more chance there is that children will develop the abilities to use their imagination, to listen and to observe.

Summary
- The things that enrich our lives are often things which arise out of our own creative efforts or those of other people, yet in our schools the expressive aspects of learning have a low status. In our settings for young children we can remedy this by ensuring that creative development is as important to us as cognitive development.
- Young children need as many opportunities as they can get to try to describe and represent their ideas and feelings.
- When children are engaged in representing and re-representing their thoughts and feelings, they are involved in solving problems, in selecting appropriate tools and materials, in cognitive development.
- The journey the child takes in representing thoughts and feelings is as important as – or even, some would argue, more important than – the final destination. In other words, although the product matters, it may well be the process that is important to the child.
- Children need to experience and explore painting and drawing, music, movement and dance, gesture and mime, storytelling and imaginative play. These should be regarded as some of the 'hundred languages' of children.
- The role of the adult is, as ever, complex. It involves setting up the environment and resources; modelling; using language to scaffold learning; offering help and advice where needed; tuning in to what it is the child is paying attention to; intervening sensitively.

Chapter 8

Ensuring equality of access and opportunity

Meeting the diverse needs of children is an underpinning principle of both the Foundation Stage and the Early Years Foundation Stage, and of all good early years practice. Ensuring that all children – whatever their background, their experience, their gender, their culture, their religion, their ability – are offered equality of access and opportunity to the curriculum and to your time is something most practitioners strive to achieve. It may seem impossible to imagine how you can do this when faced with a new group of perhaps twenty-eight young children, but if you apply the principles of good early years practice by starting with a knowledge of the children in your group (who they are, where they come from, what languages they speak, what experiences they may have had) and keep in mind each individual when planning, you will find that it is possible.

You will want to think about the items in this list and use these as a blueprint for what you will do:

- Plan opportunities that build on and extend children's knowledge, experience, interests and skills, and remember that in order to do this you have to know as much as possible about every child.
- Ensure that the opportunities help build children's self-esteem and confidence.
- Use a wide range of teaching strategies that are directly related to children's observed and assessed needs and to their interests.
- Set up an environment free of harassment where racial, religious, disability and gender stereotypes are challenged.
- Hear, respect and value the contributions of all.
- Reflect the diversity within the group, the community and the wider society in all the resources and activities.
- Monitor the progress of individual children and seek appropriate help and support where needed.

In provision, in planning and in review we need to think very carefully about children who have special educational needs or disabilities; about children who have English as an additional language; about children from various ethnic groups; and about girls and boys. We need to ask some difficult questions, including whether your provision automatically addresses the needs of all children or whether some of what are regarded as 'the truths' about early childhood include some myths which may be damaging. If you are particularly interested in this, you might want to read Glenda MacNaughton's book *Rethinking Gender in Early Childhood Education* (2000).

Politically correct or educationally essential?

Have a quick look around your room and ask yourself what it feels like to be a girl, a black child, a child from a working-class family, a child who is a refugee, a child whose home language is not English. Can you, as this child, find things that are familiar? Do you see images of children like you? Of families like yours? Do you see examples of the alphabets and scripts you see at home or in your community?

Why bother to consider issues of equality and access? You might want to jot down why you think it is important.

There are many reasons. Some of these are personal or professional in nature (as where, for example, you believe that you have a professional duty to cater for all the children you care for), or even moral and humane in intention (as where, for example, you believe that as a human being it is incumbent upon you to make sure that all children are treated equally). Many are actually grounded in legal requirements. In other words, considering the opportunities for all children is not something you can just choose to do in order to be 'right on' or politically correct. You have a legal obligation to do so under several acts.

The Children Act 1989 states that 'Children have a right to an environment which facilitates their development' and then goes on to address children's rights in terms of their sense of identity, which includes the right to individuality, respect, dignity and freedom from discrimination. If, in answering the questions that started this section, you felt that some children in your group might not feel that their particular sense of identity was overtly respected, you need to question whether you are, indeed, offering genuine equality of access and opportunity. The Children Act 2004 tightens up on the protection of children through introducing things like a new inspection framework, joint area reviews, and so on.

Every Child Matters (2004), already mentioned in Chapter 3, is a piece of legislation that seeks to maximise opportunities and minimise risks for all children. It is responsible for multi-agency approaches, extended day schemes and the appointment of a Children's Commissioner in England.

The Rumbold Report (Department of Education and Science 1990) insists that each institution should have a policy outlining aims and objectives based on a clearly articulated philosophy shared by educators and parents. This should incorporate a policy on equal opportunities for children and adults, encompassing gender, race, class and disability, which promotes an under-standing of cultural and physical diversity and challenges stereotypes and which is responsive to local needs.

You can see from all this that you need to have a policy on anti-discrimination or equity which you, as a group of practitioners, have agreed on and which you have shared with both children and parents. This policy needs to look at a number of issues, which could include the following:

- Your own *attitudes and beliefs and prejudices*. This is the essential starting point. You cannot devise and implement a policy on equal opportunities until you have examined and sometimes challenged your own views and ideas.
- A clear *understanding of the children in your care* – their home backgrounds, previous experiences, religious and cultural values, languages spoken, and other aspects of experience.
- A survey of *the resources you provide* in order to examine them for stereo-typical images and for monocultural or monolingual bias. In other words, do the books, jigsaws and pictures show positive images of girls, of black children, of children with disabilities, of boys, of working-class children? Can children find examples of their home languages in the books or tapes or wall displays in your room? Are images of Africa, for example, true to life, or do they depict Africa as a place where wild animals roam and people live in mud huts?
- A survey of *the activities you offer* in order to assess whether they invite all children to partake or in some way suggest that certain activities are only open to certain children. Obvious examples are areas like the home corner (do boys play there?) and the block play area (do girls play there?).
- An exploration of *how you handle incidents* like name-calling, bullying and teasing. Have you all agreed on a policy and do you all implement it equally?
- A consideration of *attitudes* within your setting. Ask yourself these ques-tions: Do children feel valued? Do their parents feel valued? Are children beginning to be tolerant of the feelings of others? Do you foster coopera-tion rather than competition?
- A consideration of *how parents are involved* in the work of your setting.

Reading through this list, you might believe that providing a curriculum based on meeting the observed needs of all the children in your group – a developmentally appropriate curriculum – will ensure that you offer equality of access and opportunity. But do remember that you need to take account of your own educational training, your understanding of each child, the strategies and resources you use, the views of parents, the views of children and the views of colleagues and peers. There is a growing unease about the assumption that a developmentally appropriate programme (DAP) which is based on a very Western view of childhood, of children and of learning is without question the one to be applied at all times to all children. We need to stop and remind ourselves that children growing up in developing countries also learn and develop, and we need to learn respect for views that differ from ours.

Think about the three small case studies that follow and about what the experiences of the practitioners might offer them in terms of understanding particular groups in the setting.

Julian is a male practitioner working with young children. He believes that his own experiences of growing up male in this society give him a particular viewpoint which he can use to help the boys he encounters. He spends a lot of time working with parents to help children deal with anger and aggression.

Henrietta is a black nursery nurse who works alongside a white teacher. She believes that her own experiences of discrimination gives her insights the teacher doesn't have and is keen that they work in partnership for the benefit of the children.

Iclal is a Turkish speaker who came to England with no English. Her first days in school have left a vivid impression on her and she draws on this to help the children in her class who have English as an additional language. She is very clear that dealing with discrimination means going beyond multiracial education.

Where you are aware of each child as an individual with a unique and important history and where you seek to build on this in the activities and resources you offer, you will be providing the broad and balanced curriculum recommended in the Rumbold Report. You do, however, need to know something about how social class, gender and race can provide the basis for discrimination if you are to have an effective and meaningful equal opportunities policy.

Social class

It is a truism to say that those working with young children need to know the children well. What is sometimes ignored, however, is how this knowledge about children is acquired. Sometimes practitioners make judgements about children on spurious grounds. They judge that a child will not be successful in school, for example, if the child comes from the local council estate or if the child comes from a single-parent family or if the child's parents are unemployed. Attitudes like this reflect a deficit and stereotypical view of working-class families, and often result in a self-fulfilling prophecy. Where a practitioner assumes that a child will fail, for example, that practitioner may fail to engage properly with the child's home experience, and in this way ensures that the child does fail. There are many studies you can read to illustrate this: Walkerdine *et al.* (1989), MacGilchrist (1992), Anning and Edwards (1999).

One of the most obvious areas in which social class emerges as a factor is in terms of language. Some years ago it was believed that children coming from so-called working-class homes encountered an inferior form of language within their homes. Basil Bernstein, a sociologist, in carrying out a serious study looking at the high failure rate of working-class children in English schools, said that middle-class families used what he called an 'elaborated code' of language, while working-class families used a 'restricted code' of language. What he meant by this was that speakers using the restricted code were more dependent on the immediate context in which the language took place. Working-class children, he argued, always refer to things in the here and now, things that can be seen and touched and heard. Children exposed to the elaborated code, on the other hand, were able to move away from this and were not dependent on a shared context in order to communicate. Now, since the language used in schools and in education is often about things that are not to do with the here and now and are not dependent on the current context, working-class children are at a disadvantage. This type of view – that of citing the blame for failure at school with the child and the child's family – is a deficit view and one that has been severely challenged since Bernstein's work. You have come across the work of Tizard and Hughes and of Gordon Wells and will know that they found that all homes provide language which enables children to talk, to think, to solve problems and to communicate.

Despite all this, deficit views of working-class families still prevail, and it is still a fact that working-class children do less well within the English and Welsh educational system than those from more privileged homes. What you need to ensure in your setting is that you show respect for the language brought to the setting by the children and do not make assumptions about them based on how they speak. You might like to shift the focus to the language used by you and by others in the setting, ensuring that you talk about real things in meaningful situations rather than relying on too much questioning.

Language

Throughout the United Kingdom there are many children who arrive at schools and settings having languages other than English. Some of these children are monolinguals (speakers of one language); many are bilingual or multilingual (speaking more than one language). It is an incredible fact that even today, in some places, children like these are regarded as 'knowing nothing' – purely because they are unable to fully comprehend or communicate with the adults in the school or setting. As a result, they are often offered a curriculum which is narrow and teaching approaches which are inappropriate. You will realise that these children are eager to learn English: they need it in order to survive in the classroom, the playground, the garden, the lunch room. And they will learn it at an incredible rate through playing with peers, watching television, listening to stories, engaging in activities in which the meaning is clear. What they don't need is to be withdrawn from class with other speakers of English as an additional language, in order to be 'taught' English out of context.

Good practitioners treat these children, their families and communities and languages with respect. They go to great pains to ensure that the languages spoken are evident in the setting (where possible) and they do not ask parents to refrain from speaking to their children in their first language. Rather, they recognise that it is important for the self-esteem of the children and for their relationships with others in their community to maintain their first language while they learn English. In the best practice there is evidence of the considerable knowledge these children already have about language *per se* (which we call metalinguistic knowledge) to be used as a resource within the setting. You may have come across the wonderful work of Eve Gregory and Charmian Kenner in relation to this.

Think about these case studies (Kenner 2004b, pp. 90–102) and in each one consider what it is about language itself that the child demonstrates awareness of:

Meera, aged three, was being taught only English by her mother, but Gujarati was spoken at home and she often encountered her mother writing in Gujarati to her grandmother. On one occasion she climbed on a chair to do some writing beneath her mother's Gujarati script on a poster for the nursery. She said, 'I want my Gujarati' and 'I write like my mum.'

Tala goes to Arabic school and when she tried to show her classmates how to write, she told them to start on the right-hand side of the page and she commented on some grammatical features of Arabic such as male and female verb endings.

Selina goes to Chinese school and she told her classmates that Chinese has words instead of an alphabet.

These children are not unusual. They clearly have learned a great deal about how their own language or languages work and are able to articulate this knowledge as they try to teach their monolingual friends something about their languages. Meera, for example, knows that there are different writing systems for her two languages. She wants to own both of them and she wants to be able to write like her mother. These are quite sophisticated concepts for a three-year-old. Tala knows that written English goes from left to right whereas Arabic goes from right to left. She realises that the languages are different in that Arabic requires different verb endings for different nouns. Selina recognises that there is no Chinese alphabet as such and that most Chinese characters represent a whole English word.

Gender

The process of learning about gender begins very early. Weis and Worobey (1991) believe that before the age of three, children have already developed what they call 'scripts for their gender'. When you watch the children in your setting at play you may observe clear gender preferences in terms of what the boys and girls play with, who they play with and how they play. But the fact that these gender preferences have already started developing does not mean that practitioners should be content to let them continue. Ways need to be found to allow those children who wish to explore alternative ways of playing and acting to do so. Certainly practitioners need to be aware of their own attitudes to gender and to watch carefully the models they offer and the language they use.

You may like to think about the contradiction implied when we say that children are active learners and when we say that children are socialised, at a very early age, into gender-specific roles. The latter is one of the myths we spoke of earlier in this chapter. It is important to always think of the individual child with regard to the social context within which that child learns and develops. Walkerdine *et al.* (1989) and Davies (1989) both see individuals as being both complex and multiple, and say that every individual constantly creates and recreates him- or herself through the different experiences, situations, interactions and discourses that individual encounters. This is a hopeful view and one that suggests that we should not describe girls as always being 'passive', for example. Girls may be passive in certain situations or with certain people, but if we allow ourselves to see them as 'complex and multiple', we will see that, in their play, they are often engaged in sorting out a power struggle with boys. They are acting out the power relationships they have observed and often challenging them. Just watch the girls in your home corner to see how powerful they can be.

The argument goes that simply providing things to attract girls to the construction area or boys to the home corner is not enough. What researchers suggest is that those working with young children need to pay close attention to the struggle children go through in their play and talk as they construct their own identities and learn who they are and where they are positioned. Through adult role-modelling, the use of drama and story, and through positive intervention, both boys and girls can gently be challenged and powerfully supported as they come to an understanding of who they want to be.

'Race'/ethnicity

Historically, in Western Europe in particular, there has been a view that one race of people is genetically superior to another, a view that culminated in the extermination of six million Jews under Hitler's Nazi regime. Genocide and 'ethnic cleansing' continue to be tragic events in today's world. Indeed, the world seems even more polarised than it did at the beginning of this millennium. In Britain the many groups of people who have come in from other countries have encountered active discrimination and prejudice: they have been encouraged to lose their cultures and languages in order to be assimilated into the host culture; they have been feted and treated as 'exotic' in some attempts at multiculturalism. Siraj-Blatchford (1994) argues that the only acceptable approach for those working with young children and their families is one which is genuinely anti-racist and is prepared to examine racial inequality on an institutional and on a personal level.

The colour of a person's skin is significant. It is not something that can be ignored or glossed over. Not all children are the same, and it is deeply insulting to treat all children as though they were. Very young children are aware of difference, and it is important that they have the opportunity to express their observations about difference and to come to an understanding that difference is something to celebrate and not something to jeer at or ignore. Young children, in coming to define their own identity, are inevitably influenced by other people's perceptions of them. If you are white and part of the white majority, your whiteness is not something you are acutely aware of. But if you are black and part of a black minority, your very blackness is part of what defines you.

Offering a curriculum which is multicultural is a start, but it does not go far enough if you are genuinely concerned to ensure equality of access and opportunity. What is required is ensuring that the community you create within your setting is one in which children can pursue their discovery of concepts of fairness and justice. Paley (1995) showed that young children are passionate enquirers and that their fears relate primarily to things like being left out, feeling inadequate and being unfairly treated. Paley suggests that through story (and by story she means the acting out of real or imaginary situations through play and talk), children can address these very deep concerns and come to very real understandings.

We will look now at Rainbow Playgroup's Equity Policy, which was revised in March 2006. The playgroup is committed to revising its policies regularly. This is the second revision of its original policy. It is keeping to its original agreement of revising and updating its work around anti-discrimination. As you read the policy, please remember that, for the staff, the process of agreeing the policy was more important than the policy itself. Also remember that a policy as a piece of paper is worthless. It is its implementation and continual review which gives it life and meaning.

Rainbow Playgroup Equity Policy

This is our annual revision of the policy and has involved discussion at staff in-service training, with parents and with community leaders. The process of revision took three months.

Aims

1 We aim to ensure that our environment is visually and emotionally welcoming to both children and their parents/carers. We have many different groups in our community and as these change we need to ensure that the images and languages displayed reflect our communities.

2 We base our curriculum on the Curriculum Guidance for the Foundation Stage and aim to provide learning opportunities which will allow children to build on their previous experience; to extend their knowledge and skills; to foster their own interests; to help build their sense of identity and their self-esteem and their own confidence in themselves as learners.

3 We aim to use a wide range of teaching strategies, based on what we know about each child through observation.

4 We aim to promote talking and language, including as many of the languages spoken by our children as we can, in all the activities we offer.

5 We aim to offer a safe environment free of harassment in which the contributions of all children are valued explicitly.

6 We aim to challenge any racial, religious, disability and gender stereotypes and ensure that our resources are free of these.

7 We aim to ensure that no incident of bullying is allowed to pass unnoticed or unchallenged.

continued on next page

8 We aim to use materials and activities that positively reflect diversity and are free from discrimination and stereotyping.

9 We aim to promote respect for others through our own attitudes to the children, their parents and one another.

10 We aim to promote play as the primary mode of learning since where children can follow their own interests they are more likely to become deeply immersed in what they are doing. But we recognise that children will learn also from being read to or reading themselves; from exploration and investigation and from activities that may be adult-directed.

11 We aim to promote cooperation and collaboration rather than competition.

12 We aim to ensure that we are alert to any signs of discrimination and, as a staff, do not ignore such incidents or tacitly support them in any way.

13 We aim to form close and respectful relationships with parents in order to build a partnership with them which involves both parties in listening and hearing the views expressed.

Operating the policy

1   We will organise the playgroup so that our commitment to equality of access and opportunity is evident to all.

2   We will plan for and monitor the activities to ensure that no child is denied access to any activity on offer. We will also monitor our time to ensure that no child or children dominate our time at the expense of other children.

3   The resources we use and the activities we plan will reflect aspects of the community we serve. All activities will include resources and artefacts which will be familiar to the children and allow them to build on their prior experience.

4   We will continue to invite parents, carers and community members in to share their own skills, expertise and experience with us.

5   We will consider the very particular needs of children with special educational needs in our planning, ensuring that we consider things like access, resources and support.

6   We will explain the policy to new parents, using translators and interpreters when necessary.

7   We will plan our meetings with parents at a time to suit their needs.

continued on next page

8   Our settling-in procedures will include inviting parents to bring a friend or older sibling to help with communication in English.
9   We will not allow any racist or sexist incident to pass unchallenged.

NOTE: *This policy will be reviewed each year and rewritten when there are significant changes. Any parent/carer wishing to contribute their views or ideas is invited to use the 'comments' box in the entrance hall. You may remain anonymous if you choose!*

Children with special educational needs

Within any setting there will be children who have special needs and some who have special educational needs. Children who have English as an additional language may have special needs with regard to acquiring English but their needs will be different from those of children who need specialist help within the education system. It is vital – in fact it is obligatory – for you to know what the needs of the children in your care are and to know exactly what your responsibilities are in dealing with these children.

In your setting you will have children whose development varies enormously. You may have a very tall four-year-old whose language development does not seem equivalent to that of other four-year-olds. You may have a tiny four-year-old who is extremely articulate, but who has difficulty with fine motor control. Children, as we know, vary enormously in their rate of development, and in our zeal to describe children, we sometimes label them as having 'special needs' or as being 'slow', 'naughty' or 'average'. Labels such as these suggest that we know something impossible – namely, that there is such a thing as 'average' or 'normal'. More importantly, these labels are usually negative and not very informative or precise and, what is more, they often become attached to the child. A child who is labelled at an early age as being a failure in some way carries the additional disadvantage of having to overcome this label.

At the other extreme, however, is the fact that the early detection of particular difficulties allows for early intervention. This means that you, working with young children, are in a position to be alert to signs of problems that young children may be having (perhaps only temporarily) and know how to respond to these. This is a tremendous responsibility, but English law now provides a framework to help all those involved with children to know what to do. The revised Code of Practice, implemented in January 2002, provides a framework for developing strong partnerships between parents, schools and settings, local education authorities and health and social services. It emphasises the rights of children, allowing their voices to be heard, and promotes a consistent approach to meeting children's special educational needs (SEN). Here are the principles upon which the code is based:

- A child with special needs should have these needs met.
- The special needs of children will normally be met in mainstream schools.
- The views of children should be sought and taken into account.
- Parents have a vital role to play in supporting their child's education.
- Children with SEN should be offered full access to a broad, balanced and relevant education, including, where appropriate, the curriculum for the Foundation Stage and the National Curriculum.

Early years settings are required to take note of the Code of Practice, particularly in terms of planning through Early Years Action and Action Plus for children who do not yet have statements. It is relatively rare for such young children to have need of a statutory assessment made by the local education authority.

The revised Code of Practice places the emphasis for support on schools, trying to keep children within mainstream schooling, but with staff being able to call upon outside resources and specialist expertise. This is a graduated approach, with the teacher being able to use an array of strategies to support the child before consulting the school's Special Educational Needs Coordinator (SENCO) or before moving on to register concerns at the level of School Action Plans.

The first stage of the process is where the practitioners develop a concern about a child and then pay particular attention to how that child is progressing, using a range of ways of supporting the child, offering differentiated work and using supportive intervention strategies. The practitioner starts to keep detailed records based on observations, highlighting both strengths and weaknesses and listing what has been done. If the practitioner is unhappy about the child's development, the SENCO should be consulted and the progress of the child reviewed. It is at this stage that a specially drawn up Individual Education Plan (IEP) might be introduced. It is possible that the review may conclude that the child needs specialist help over and above that available in the school or setting, and the child's name could then be put on the school or setting's Special Education Needs Register at what is called School Action. Hopefully, parents will have been involved and consulted at all points up to this stage, but it is here that the school or setting has a duty to inform parents that special educational provision is being sought for the child.

Clearly, the child concerned is in need of some special attention in order that what is deemed 'adequate progress' is made. This is a tricky concept, but the Code of Practice summarises it as follows. Adequate progress is progress that:

- closes the attainment gap between the child and his or her peers;
- prevents the attainment gap getting wider;
- is similar to that of peers starting from the same baseline, but less than that of the majority of peers;
- matches or betters the child's previous progress;
- demonstrates an improvement in self-help, social or personal skills;
- demonstrates an improvement in the child's behaviour.

You will see from this list that attention is not solely on the child's intellectual or cognitive gains, but also on his or her independence, ability to interact or show appropriate feelings, and on the child's behaviour.

You will certainly have a copy of the Code of Practice in your school or setting and you will also have a SENCO to whom you can turn for additional advice and support. Primarily, as someone working with children in the Foundation Stage, or even earlier, your prime responsibility is to be attentive to children who demonstrate behavioural, social or cognitive difficulties that seem out of line to you. It is vital that you act on this as required and liaise closely with parents.

Much emphasis is now placed on keeping children who have particular needs or difficulties within mainstream settings. This model of inclusion is one that offers benefits for all children, who learn to live with, respect and support children who are different in some ways. It is also a model that requires adequate staffing, appropriate staff training and generous funding, and these, sadly, are not always available, placing enormous strain on staff.

Summary
- Avoid labelling children.
- Observe children carefully and pay attention to any child whose behaviour in any way concerns you.
- Be aware of the requirements of the revised Code of Practice.
- Publish your policy on how your setting identifies children with special educational needs and sets about attempting to meet these.
- Identify a member of staff (the SENCO) who will take particular responsibility for this area.
- Liaise closely with parents, keeping them informed, and treat them with respect and sensitivity.

Working towards equity and equality

In this chapter we have started to examine the responsibility that all those working with young children have – morally, professionally and legally – to address issues of equality and equity for all children. This is an area that many practitioners find difficult to deal with because it sometimes forces them to face issues concerning their own views, beliefs and values. We all like to believe that we are without prejudice, yet confronting our innermost feelings sometimes reveals surprising and damaging things.

Within your setting you need to remember that you are empowered to create your own community. This community is bound to be influenced by the pressures and demands of the wider society, but it is possible to create a community which is socially just. You are in a position to influence the development of young children as social beings, initially within the social community of the setting or classroom, but equipping them to later look for justice in the wider community. Recall the work of people like Paley and Dyson, who, through story and role-play, allowed the children to create their own communities within the classroom or setting.

In all probability you will already have started doing some things towards achieving this goal. You may have looked at your resources in order to ensure that the images they offer are not stereotypes but show males and females and people from different cultures doing everyday, ordinary things. Images like this will allow the children both to build on their previous experience and to develop a sense of identity which they can be proud of. You will probably have thought about how you can support children whose first language is not English in continuing to use that language, but also in acquiring English. You may have thought of providing books in languages other than English; of using story props to allow children into the meaning of the stories you tell and read; of displaying the alphabets and scripts used by the children and their families. You may have paid some attention to things like gender equality by considering what resources you offer in the home corner to encourage boys to play there; how you encourage girls to take active roles in outdoor play and block and construction play. You may have started to work closely with parents in order that you are able to understand and respect their views and explain yours to them in ways in which they can understand.

These aspects of ensuring equity and equality are important, but, in a sense, they are the ones that are relatively easy to do. In order that your policy has some 'teeth', however, there are some difficult things you have to do – and since these often involve changing attitudes, they take a long time. At William Patten Infants School in Hackney in the early 1980s the staff set about developing an anti-racist policy. After much debate and heart-searching, it was decided that the starting point had to be with the views of the staff. The staff split into two groups and each group met separately under the leadership of one of the teachers. The reason for the split was that those members of staff who were not teachers felt intimidated by the teachers and requested to be allowed to meet on their own. Each group met regularly over a long period of time and the purpose was for each person, in turn, to relate their life story. There was only one rule – and that was that everyone had to listen and no one was allowed to interrupt. The point of doing this was for people who had previously been somewhat suspicious of those coming from a different cultural background to discover the things they had in common and to begin to develop an understanding of oppression. In our polarised world it seems vital that those most intimately involved in the care and education of young children become prepared and able to examine and change their own views in order to create a just and fair society in microcosm.

So, addressing issues of equality involves an examination of your own attitudes and also a willingness to consider factors of power and control that operate at a level beyond that of the individual. Weiner (1985) talks of the ongoing battle for power that exists between different groups – between men and women, between black and white people, between poor and rich. Inevitably, when considering such factors, one has to adopt a stance which is essentially political, and many people find this difficult. But you, as practitioners, have an obligation to treat children as human beings and to deal with them seriously.

Think about what it is that practitioners must offer young children to help them understand the world in all its complexities. Can you add to the list below, drawn from the work of Kidner (1988)?

- The presence of adults who are prepared to look objectively at their own practice to see how it affects different groups of children.
- A curriculum that values a range of cultures, languages and lifestyles.
- The provision of learning activities which allow children to explore ideas and concepts which will allow them to come to understand racism and other forms of oppression.

Summary
- In this chapter we have taken a very brief look at serious and contentious issues relating to what experiences children may have in the schools and settings they attend. These experiences will vary, of course, from individual to individual, but it is important that children who belong to particular groups or communities or who are 'different' in any way are treated with respect and do not experience any kind of injustice or bullying.

Chapter 9

Documenting what children do

In good early years practice, practitioners pay close attention to what children do and say as they play and learn, and use this as the basis for their planning. They also use it in order to build up a picture of each child as a learner, and share their findings, formally, through reports to parents and to receiving teachers. This tracking and documenting of what children do is very important and highly skilled. Observation as a teaching tool and part of the planning cycle has been in place for many years, starting with the work of Susan Isaacs at the Maltings School. The Foundation Stage Profile (introduced in 2003) lays down a structure built partly on observation, to offer a common framework for tracking progress in the foundation stage. It replaces previous statutory baseline assessment on entry to primary school. If you are not familiar with it, you can obtain a copy by contacting the Qualifications and Curriculum Authority (www.qca.org.uk).

The Profile states the following:

- It builds on the curriculum guidance.
- It reflects the key role of skilful and well-planned observations in providing reliable assessment information on young children.
- It recognises the important contribution parents and children can make to assessment.
- It has been developed drawing on extensive expertise of a group of early years specialists – the same group as was involved in drawing up the curriculum guidance.
- It sets out a way of summarising young children's achievements at the end of the Foundation Stage and provides important information for both parents and Year 1 teachers.

This, at first glance, is a sound set of principles and reveals what appear to be well-considered views of learning. But let us take a closer look and see if the reality is as useful as the rhetoric suggests.

Assessment and assessment scales

All those working with young children are now required to assess each child's development in relation not only to the early learning goals but also to the stepping stones. Assessments are to be made on the basis of observations and knowledge of the child. By the end of the final year of the Foundation Stage, the Profile will 'sum up' that knowledge. You may want to be reminded that ongoing assessment – the type of assessment you make through focused or less formal on-the-hoof observations – is called 'formative' assessment, and it is this that you use for planning. The type of assessment that sums up what is known about a child is called summative assessment.

The early learning goals were not originally devised to be assessment scales, but the Profile has captured these early learning goals as a set of thirteen assessment scales, each of which has nine points. The early learning goals are presented individually or, in some cases, have been split or combined for ease of use. Let us take a look at the nine points below, in Table 9.1.

Those of you involved in assessing progress throughout the Foundation Stage will have to complete the Foundation Stage Profile scale booklet by the end of the reception year. In order to do this you will have to record each item the child has achieved in each scale.

There is insufficient space here to detail what it is that practitioners must do, but the Profile handbook and accompanying CD are both detailed and informative. Sadly, they do not reduce the enormous load placed on practitioners in recording the information.

Observation

In the best practice, practitioners watch children carefully and listen to what they say. They often carry a pad and pen and jot down what they see and hear.

Table 9.1 Points on the assessment scales for the early learning goals

Steps 1–3	These describe a child who is progressing towards the achievements described in the early learning goals. They are based mainly on the stepping stones. Most children will achieve these points before they achieve any of the early learning goals, but this is not universally so.
Steps 4–8	These are drawn from the early learning goals and presented in supposed order of difficulty. This comes from evidence gained in the trials of the Profile. They are not necessarily hierarchical, and a child may achieve a later point without having achieved some of the earlier ones.
Step 9	This describes a child who has achieved all the previous points and has developed beyond these in both breadth and depth.

At the end of the session or the day the trained practitioner then reads through each observation note and tries to interpret what has been seen and heard in terms of what the children demonstrate about what they know and can do. So, as you observe, some questions may be raised in your mind. The answers to these questions not only help you to understand more about the children but also give you an insight into how well you, the adult, are managing to support and extend children's learning.

Drummond (1998) says that observing children's learning is one of the most vital responsibilities of those who care for and educate children. When we observe children's amazing capacity for learning and development, it shows how much we must do in order to support, enrich and extend that learning. She goes on to say:

> Observing learning, getting close to children's minds and children's feelings, is part of our daily work in striving for quality. What we see, when we look closely, helps us to shape the present, the daily experiences of young children in all forms of early years provision. The act of observation is central to the continuous process of evaluation, as we look at what we provide and ask: is it good enough? Our careful observations of children's learning can help us make this provision better. We can use what we see to identify the strengths and weaknesses, gaps and inconsistencies, in what we provide. We can identify significant moments in a child's learning, and we can build on what we see.
>
> (1998, p. 105)

It is important in any setting to ensure that observation is systematic. By this we mean that there is some system in place to ensure that all children are assessed and that observations follow some sort of plan. All those working with young children need to be involved in the observation and assessment process. If you operate a key worker system, you will be primarily responsible for observing your key children. But in reality, in most settings, children move around so frequently that a practitioner may observe something very significant about a child who is not one of his or her key children.

How you organise to observe children will be up to you as a staff group. There is no right way, but there are ways which are more efficient than others. Clearly, you will want to observe children individually and in groups, in a range of activities and covering all six learning areas.

Think about what these examples offer:

In our playgroup each practitioner chooses to look at four children over the week. She tries to observe those children in different activities and jots down notes as she does so. Then, on Friday, when the children have gone home we all sit down and summarise what we have seen about each of the children.

If another practitioner has observed one of the target children doing something interesting, she will add her comments.

We vary what we do. At the moment we are observing the children in different areas. So my area this week is the home corner and I jot down notes about significant things that happen. Then we get together and share our observations.

We've tried everything! At one point we seemed to spend our whole time writing, and decided that that was not the best use of our time. At the moment we have organised the room so that in each area there are clipboards with pens attached, so that if something significant happens we can record it. But we each take responsibility for observing three children per week.

Through your observations you will come across incidents that can be described as 'significant moments'. These are where a child does something for the first time. If you think about your own children's development or the development of children you know well, the things that stand out in your memory may be the so-called milestones – the first word, the first step, and so on. In terms of monitoring the development of the children in your care, you are looking for evidence of the child having moved on, having taken the next step in learning and development. Here are some examples of significant moments for different children, linked, where possible, with the Assessment Scales:

> Paolo was very shy and withdrawn. I felt it was significant when I saw him approach another child, tug his arm and point to the car he was holding.
> (PSE Social Development 1)

> Boris never ever chose to look at books. It was significant when he came in one morning and headed straight for the book corner.
> (CLL Reading 1)

> Sacha, nearly six, says she read a book 'in her head'.
> (CLL Reading 9)

> Sammy, aged four, said, 'The numbers on this side of the road go up in twos.'
> (MD: Very difficult to find where this belongs, although it is clearly a significant leap in understanding about counting in twos and about pattern.)

(*Note:* PSE stands for Personal, Social and Emotional Development; CLL for Communications, Language and Literacy; and MD for Mathematical Development.)

Observation and planning

The first and most obvious thing you do with your observations is use them to plan what to offer next. In this way you are basing your planned programme on the interests and needs of the children as you have observed them. So, observation informs planning. You will remember how we talked in the last chapter about how planning based on the observed interests and needs of individual children ensures that the programme provided offers genuine equality of access and opportunity to all children. So, you are using your observations to identify what each child knows and can do, so that you can plan what you need to offer to take that child's learning forward. From your observations you will set about planning activities that are relevant and motivating for the children.

Once you have used your observations to plan what to offer next, you can also think about how to use them to build a record of the child's progress over time. Inevitably, if all members of staff are keeping notes on what they notice, you will gather a veritable mountain of paper over the days and weeks. It is here that you need to use your judgement about what is significant. I would suggest that each key worker be responsible for collecting together the bits of paper relating to her key children. She then needs to sift through them, extracting what is significant and discarding the rest. There is absolutely no point in keeping every observation note made. What you want to do is track each child's progress, and the best way of doing this is to chart the leaps in learning mentioned earlier in this chapter.

You will want to ensure that you have observation notes covering all aspects of the curriculum. Where you have been worried about a child's emotional development it is natural that your observation notes will reflect this. But the child's overall development needs to be charted and you need to ensure that you have noticed something about the child's learning across the six areas of learning.

Interpreting what you see

Writing down what you see and hear is easy enough. It is like taking a photograph or making a tape recording. You record exactly what happens. But, as we have said earlier, observations on their own are of little use. What you need to do is interpret what you see and hear so as to understand what it shows you about the child's learning and development.

Think about this example and consider what you can learn from this about what the child is paying attention to or interested in. Think, too, of what you would do to take his learning forward.

Four-year-old Abdul has recently arrived in the United Kingdom from Bangladesh and does not yet have any English. You notice that he likes to go into the book corner and sort out all the books according to size.

Do you think Abdul might be interested in size? Or perhaps in sorting things out? You cannot ever know for sure whether your assessment is correct or not, but considering what children's interests might be offers you useful ways for planning to take their learning forward. Did you think about bringing in some boxes of different sizes, inviting him to sort the books, by size, into the boxes? Did you think of reading the story – and using props to make it come alive for Abdul – of Goldilocks and the Three Bears? Did you think about introducing objects of varying sizes in the home corner as a follow-up to this – three different-sized beds, three different-sized teddies, three different-sized bowls, and so on?

Drummond cites the example of a four-year-old girl who examines shells and pebbles under several different types of magnifiers. She spends a long time bringing the lens close to her eye and then moving it away again. She then picks up a shell, examines it under the magnifier on a tripod and then holds it to each ear in turn. Then she puts the shell again under the tripod, but this time places her ear, rather than her eye, against the magnifying glass as though she were trying to magnify the sound. Drummond asks:

> Whatever was she doing? Was she ignorant? Or stupid? No, neither of these. As I watched I realised she was asking a question, not out loud, but privately, to herself. She had established that the magnifying glass made the shell look bigger, now she wanted to know 'will it make it louder?'
>
> (1998, p. 102)

Close observation allows us to make guesses about what children already know and about what their current interests are. But since we make our guesses in the light of what we already know about that particular child, and also what we know about how young children learn, these are educated guesses. So, we use what we see and hear (our observation notes) as the information or evidence we gather and then interpret this in the light of our knowledge to help us plan what we will offer next to take learning forward.

Involving parents

The *Foundation Stage Profile: Handbook* (Department for Education and Skill, 2003) considers those who are involved in the assessment process and prime among these are parents. In fact, it reminds us that a genuine partnership between practitioners and parents is one of the key principles of the Foundation Stage. It is a cliché to say that parents know more about their own child than anyone else, but like most clichés it is true. Practitioners and teachers do, of course, get to know children well, but it is important to recognise that their knowledge of any child is limited. The person who sees the child in almost every situation at almost every time of the day and year is the parent. Parents are, indeed, experts when it comes to their own child. Despite this fact, many parents are made to feel that they know nothing and that their understanding of the child may be flawed or limited. This applies particularly to parents whose first language is not English or to parents who feel threatened by the education system and by authority. These parents find it difficult to have their voices heard and tend to adopt the stance that 'Teacher and playgroup practitioners know best!'

All parents, whatever their culture, language, background, social class or gender, care about their children. Parents who send young children to a nursery or crèche or playgroup do so for many reasons: some because they feel their children will benefit from contact with other children; some because they want their children to have a head start in the education stakes; some because they need or want to work or study. But all parents want the best for their children and all parents deserve to be kept informed about how their children are making progress. Good practice in terms of building and maintaining parental participation and contribution includes the following:

- Attempts should be made by practitioners to ensure that parents are kept fully informed about what takes place at the setting through as many means as possible. These might include informal discussions and more formal things such as brochures or displays or videos which are available in the languages of the parents.
- Parents and practitioners talk together about the child and record what is said about the child's progress and achievements. This process can take place through meetings or through making a book about the child, to which the child may also contribute.
- A positive initial meeting with parents is held, which will set the tone for the coming relationship. This will take place early in the year and it is at this meeting that practitioners should seek the views of the parents about what the child has done outside of the setting. There is much to be learned from this about what the child can already do and already knows; about what the child is interested in or passionate about; about any special needs or requirements the child might have. The meeting could

become detailed enough to record favourite books or stories or routines or people. This is the ideal time to find out about the language or languages the child can speak and perhaps even read or write. Within the *Foundation Stage Profile: Handbook* (Department for Education and Skills 2003) there are a number of prompt questions which practitioners may use or may give to parents who are unable to attend a meeting. But do take care here and remember that not all parents will be literate, certainly not in English.

- Good ongoing exchange of information is necessary. In some settings this is done through a home/school diary or a reading book which goes back and forth from home to school and where comments are written and read. It can be done through regular review meetings or through special events like joint book-choosing sessions. Although the handbook makes mention of offering parents advice on activities to do at home, there is not the space here to discuss this, which is a contentious issue and one that needs to be handled with great sensitivity in order not to impose one way of parenting on others. You can read more about this on p. 103 of the handbook.

- Finally, the Profile should be shared with parents through the statutory reporting requirements.

In the Italian nurseries described in an earlier chapter, a great deal of work goes into keeping parents informed about their children's progress. Each child has a plastic wallet up on the wall, and staff put into these wallets brief comments about what the child has done that day. For parents of very young children, this information makes them feel involved in their children's progress. No parent wants to miss their own child's first step or first word. Parents of older children are equally entitled to learn of their children's progress. What is more, they will notice changes in their child's behaviour and learning at home and can add these to the child's profile.

Involving children

Children do need to be involved in assessing their own progress; it is a vital part of learning. We all know that, as learners, we often need to have our achievements validated by others. Children, too, need to have this happen, and in good practice this is what achieved through successful, skilled and focused scaffolding.

Think about what the child learns from scaffolding or from non-focused praise. Do you think they are the same thing?

Ciarron has completed her picture. She takes it to the teacher, who says, 'Lovely'; and puts a smiley face on it.

Arhad has drawn a very complex picture and takes it to the teacher, who spends a long time looking at it and then says, 'You worked at that for a very long time. I was watching you and I thought how clever you are to be able to concentrate for such a long time.'

Rafael won a Star of the Week certificate for getting ten stars during the week.

Malika managed to put on her shoes by herself after being in the sandpit. The nursery nurse said, 'Wow, Malika. You put on your shoes all by yourself. What a big girl you are becoming.'

Where the response from the adult is in the form of some extrinsic reward – something not integral to the situation – the child learns little from it. Rewarding stars or smiley faces or certificates merely focuses on the end product and not on the process. Where the adult manages to recognise what it was the child was paying attention to and then comments on that, the child is able to build on this recognition. Self-awareness is a vital part of learning.

You can seek the views of children in many ways – through talking to them or inviting them to make drawings or draw pictures. What seems important is to get children to talk about what they enjoyed doing; what they feel they did well; how they arrived at solutions or answers to problems; what strategies they used; whether they worked alone or with others; and so on.

Here, as illustrations, are a comment made by Farida in discussion with her teacher, Annie, and a comment from Farida's mother giving her views on how the child is getting on:

Parent's comments: 'I am happy with how Farida is getting on. She likes the playgroup and is looking forward to going to school. At home she looks at books a lot and sings lots of songs. She also likes to write.'

Child's comments: 'Look, Annie. I made a pattern.'
'Annie, I can write my name and my brother's name now. It goes F A R O U K – like this!'

Summative assessment and reports

The type of assessment we have been looking at is known as formative assessment. It is what you do all the time in your work in order to ensure both that the children are making progress and that what you are offering is providing the necessary challenge and support to ensure that this happens. Formative assessment is crucial to any educational enterprise. Summative assessment is the type of assessment that summarises a child's achievements at a particular point in time. The most obvious example of summative assessment is the end-of-year report. You will remember from your own school days how getting the school report could either be an occasion for celebration or one for misery. School reports used to consist, often, of a mark or grade accompanied by a very brief and bald comment – something like 'Judy has done very well at PE this term' or 'Marcus needs to try harder'. These comments gave parents no indication of exactly what the child had achieved over the year. Nor did they give any indication of what particular problems might be – or any recommended course of action.

Nowadays, summative assessments are better in that they do try to summarise all that practitioners or teachers have found from their formative assessments over a period of time. There is a legal requirement on all schools and settings to write an end-of-year report for parents.

Here, as an example, is a report for Farida (whom you met in the previous sub-section):

Personal, social and emotional development: Farida started the year very timidly. She tended to play alone and was often observed to be rather withdrawn. Over the year, as her self-esteem and ability to use English have developed, so has her confidence. As she moves into the reception class she has already met a number of the early learning goals. She is interested and motivated to learn and confident to try new activities. She can concentrate for long periods of time and has formed good relationships with both adults and other children. She understands a lot about right and wrong and is very independent. She likes to work as part of a group and has developed a particular friendship with Harinder.

Communication, language and literacy: Farida has made great strides in this learning area and again already meets several of the early learning goals. She listens with enjoyment to songs and rhymes and knows many by heart. She can retell some stories and her favourites are 'Peepo' and 'Brown Bear'. She can recognise her own name and those of her friends and knows that, in English, print is read from left to right and top to bottom. She enjoys making up stories and knows the difference between writing and drawing. She often chooses to write letters, books, cards or to fill in blank forms. She can write her own name and those of her brother and sister.

Mathematical development: Farida counts reliably to twelve and recognises the symbols to 10. She enjoys making patterns in her drawing and in her play with blocks and also enjoys exploring space. She uses the language of

continued on next page

mathematics very well (high, low, underneath, heavy, etc.). She uses her developing mathematical ideas to solve practical problems that she encounters in her play.

Creative development: Farida enjoys choosing materials and tools to make things. She likes exploring colour and shape and enjoys painting, using clay and making things in the workshop area. She explores colour, texture and shape in both two and three dimensions. She enjoys singing and dancing and spends much of her time in complex role-play both inside and out. She likes to play the musical instruments.

Physical development: Farida has overcome her initial nervousness and now enjoys playing outdoors and in, moving with confidence and imagination, with increased control and coordination. She can run, jump, balance, catch and throw. She uses a wide range of tools with great skill and manages fine tools like pens and pencils effectively.

Knowledge and understanding of the world: Farida is curious and interested in many things. She often asks questions and enjoys investigating objects and materials using all her senses. She talks about patterns and differences and similarities. She often tries things out and discusses what is happening. She is willing to take risks. She knows a great deal about her own language and culture and shares with adults and children with whom she feels comfortable. Farida has made great strides and has been a delightful member of the nursery community. She will enjoy learning in the same way in the reception class.

A report like this should be comprehensible to the parents, written as it is in everyday language rather than in educational jargon and saying clearly what it is that the child can do and has achieved. The same report sent to the receiving teacher will give her or him some indication of what the child has already done and what the child's interests and strengths are. A teacher receiving Farida's report would be unlikely to assume that Farida knows nothing about reading and writing, for example. There is clear evidence of what she already knows, and this provides the teacher with some indication of where to start her or his programme for this child.

Summary

- Everyone involved in the education and care of young children has a professional obligation to document children's progress. This is a difficult task and one that many practitioners find daunting.
- The only way you can know how children are progressing is to observe them as they play and to write down your observations.
- Everyone involved with the child should contribute to this.
- The observation notes on their own are only of use if you analyse them to find what they show you about what the child already knows and can do, what the child is interested in and/or paying attention to.
- On the basis of this you can evaluate both the child's progress and how well you are meeting the child's needs.
- Observation then suggests what you should plan next in order that children can take the next step in their learning.
- Parents and children should be involved in the assessment process.
- A good programme of formative assessment can lead to summative assessment which carries information that is meaningful to parents and of use to receiving teachers or practitioners.
- There is a legal requirement to write end-of-year or end-of-stage reports for parents and receiving teachers.

Chapter 10

Partnerships with parents

You can be left in little doubt that it is generally considered to be a 'good thing' for parents and carers to be intimately involved with the schools and settings which care for and educate their children. *Birth to Three Matters*, the *Curriculum Guidance for the Foundation Stage* and the *Foundation Stage Profile: Handbook* all remind us of this. Parents, we all know and appreciate, are children's first educators. Current UK government thinking places parents high on the agenda, talking about ways of helping parents (particularly mothers) go back to work or study and offering them that 'golden' word: choice. Indeed, in December 2004 the government published a policy document called *Choice for Parents: The Best Start for Children* and described the policy as a ten-year strategy for childcare. The goals of the policy are laudable: more money, more training, more inter-agency work. The policy arises out of the research mentioned in an earlier chapter (Daycare Trust 2004) and the Effective Provision of Pre-School Education (EPPE) Project. Here are some of the things being proposed:

- The setting up of children's centres where the youngest children are brought together in one setting so that there is care and education for babies, toddlers and pre-schoolers.
- The leaders of these children's centres to be offered training through a one-year programme focusing on leadership (currently being trialled).
- By 2008 there are supposed to be children's centres serving 2,500 communities.
- The setting up of childminding networks to link childminders caring for children in homes rather than settings to be linked into the system.
- The setting up of extended day programmes for schools, allowing parents to be offered care for their children beyond the hours of the traditional school day.
- Funding for childcare through working tax credits which is aimed to go beyond the current figure of £135 per week for a single child and £300 for two children in a family.

- Joined-up services for families.
- A proper qualifications strategy for childcare workers.
- Attention paid to parental leave and to flexible working.

It is up to you to decide whether this approach takes seriously raising the status of childcare as a profession, of childcare workers within society, of children within our culture. Sceptics might suggest that the policy has more to do with getting parents back to work to boost the economy than about offering universal, free quality care and education to all children whose parents want it.

In terms of parental participation there is a wealth of documented evidence showing that where parents and practitioners work closely together, children thrive. It is imperative that in any setting a genuine two-way partnership is established. This means that information goes from setting to home and from home to setting. It means that any setting spends time establishing some ground rules about how to set up such a partnership in order that the following principles are followed:

- Practitioners show respect for and understanding of the particular role of each parents as primary educator.
- Practitioners talk to parents about their expectations of the setting and explain to parents the curriculum, the routines, the ethos and the philosophy.
- Practitioners talk to parents about their child – about his or her development and about any concerns they may have.
- Settling-in arrangements are thoughtful and allow time for children to be secure.
- All parents are made welcome and can see evidence of their culture and languages in the setting.
- The particular knowledge, skills and expertise of parents is used to support the learning activities on offer.
- Parents are kept informed about what is happening on a daily, weekly and longer-term basis.
- Parents are kept informed about what the children are doing and learning.
- Parents have the opportunity to contribute to assessments made of their own children (to records and profiles).
- Parents are invited to read with children and play games with them at home so that the divisions between home and school are minimised.

Read and think about this account of how seven-month-old Sam was inducted into his nursery which is part of the fantastic early years provision in Reggio Emilia in Italy.

Sam's mother, Jenny Leask, tells us that their first meeting was with the two full-time teachers who would be with him, together with the school cook, who was regarded as a key figure in the school. The parents were asked detailed questions about Sam as a little boy. What did he like doing? How did he like to be held? How did he behave when he was tired? The answers they gave were written down, and when Sam started, three weeks later, his parents found this little biography of their son and his photograph displayed on the wall alongside similar little histories of the other new children. Displayed too were details of the parents: names, dates of birth, professions, etc. 'It dawned on us that we were part of that group too, about to become part of the school.'

If you want to know more about the care given to settling-in procedures and parental partnerships, do read Leask's article in *Experiencing Reggio Emilia* (Abbott and Nutbrown 2001).

Parents and schools: a potted history

The role of parents with regard to the education of their children out of the home has a long and difficult history. There were those who held that teachers were professionals who knew best about what young children needed and that parents should be happy to hand over their young children without question into such capable hands. Home and school were kept separate, with no recognition of the fact that learning begins at home and that parents are fundamentally involved in the education process.

When the importance of the role of parents began to be recognised, it was in the sense that 'good' parents are able to help their children's learning by supporting what happens in the school or nursery. 'Bad' parents were seen to hold children back. For several decades it was believed that it was the role of schools and teachers to educate these 'inadequate' parents (who were invariably poor or black) and to compensate for the perceived inadequacies of the home. This view was exemplified in programmes like the Head Start programme in the United States. Even the Plowden Report in 1967, which advocated partnership with parents, saw the role of parents as limited to that of raising funds and being informed about their children's progress and development by teachers through regular meetings. So, parents continued to play a largely passive role – receiving information rather than contributing to children's progress. In the 1980s a different view of parents emerged, and much of that was to do with the work of researchers like Tizard and Hughes (1984) and Gordon Wells (1987), who demonstrated effectively that most homes, regardless of socioeconomic level or other factors, provide rich learning environments. Alongside this came a recognition that parents know more about their own children than teachers and playgroup workers do, and if children are to be offered rich learning experiences in the nursery and playgroup which allow them to build on what they already know, this expertise of parents needed to be made accessible to all those working with the child. More recently still, a complex view of parents has arisen. There is a recognition that parents need to be involved in the care and education of their children, but there is also a view of parents as being in need of knowing how to parent. This is a contentious and a patronising view – one that suggests that someone, somewhere knows what makes a 'good' parent. The reality is that ways of parenting are as various as ways of dressing or cooking or dancing. Economic factors, educational levels, position in society will all affect how well parents are able to parent, and it is important to remember that parents will, almost by definition, want what is best for their children. It follows from that that they will do the best that they can. That seems a basic principle for all practitioners to hold to.

The changing role of parents is reflected at the official level. Under the 1944 Education Act parents were seen as having a duty to ensure that their children received education suitable to their age and ability. The Taylor Report (Department of Education and Science 1977) emphasised parental responsibility, but did recognise that individual parents might need to band together in order to have a collective voice. The report advocated that parents should have equal representation with teachers, the local education authority and the local community on school governing bodies. The 1980 Education Act, which followed this report, only partly implemented these recommendations, and it was only with the 1986 Education (No. 2) Act that parents were given equal representation with local education authority members. The Act further required that all schools furnish parents with an annual report and hold an annual meeting for parents.

The most important piece of legislation recognising that parents have rights as well as responsibilities came in the late 1970s with the Warnock Report (Department of Education and Science 1978), which looked at children with special needs. This report recommended that teachers and schools should be required to seek the full involvement of parents, and the notion of parental–school partnerships really emerged. In the late 1980s, with the publication of the 1988 Education Act, the role of parents shifted again, with the emphasis now being placed on parental choice. This notion of parental choice is a key theme underpinning much of current government legislation – as you will realise when you consider relatively recent legislation regarding nursery education. It is exemplified in the Parent's Charter (1994). This document suggests that parents can influence schools significantly through their right to choose schools for their children. It also suggests that parents become 'active partners with the school and its teachers'. This approach shifts education to a new arena – that of the marketplace – and places responsibilities on parents to exercise their rights as consumers.

Other laws have been touched on throughout this book and earlier in this chapter.

You might like to consider this in depth and decide whether you feel that education is best situated in the marketplace and whether the concept of parents as consumers is the best way forward in establishing good relationships. You can see how parents, over the past thirty years, have been given some rights individually to be involved with the education of their children and some collective rights in terms of serving on governing bodies, which now have increased powers.

Why involve parents?

Nowadays it is rare to find anybody who doesn't think that parental involvement in education is a 'good' thing. But defining quite why this is so is complex. Here are some suggestions, drawn from Robson (1996).

- Parents have rights and schools and settings need to be accountable to parents. The Children Act 1989 states that all parents have responsibilities towards their own children, and these include concern for their care and education. More importantly, however, is the fact that parents are their child's first educators and have a continuing concern for their child's education away from the home. This view enshrines the rights of all parents to be consulted and informed about their child's progress, and makes institutions involved in the care and education of children accountable to parents.
- Parents can have a positive effect on their children's attainment and progress. Tizard et al. (1988) showed that 97 percent of parents of children in the reception class helped them at home with reading. They had similar findings with regard to parents helping their children with mathematics. A number of schemes for involving parents more directly with their children's work in schools have revealed gains. Working-class parents are as keen and able to help their children with learning at home as more middle-class parents. The fact that all parents want their children to do well at nursery and school has important implications for how workers relate to parents.
- Parental involvement in the school can help minimise conflicts between the values of home and school. We have touched on this in earlier chapters. Since all schools and settings serve diverse communities with different value systems, the more that is known about these values and beliefs, the better the relationship between parents and workers. Where workers are able to understand and consider different styles and expectations, they are more likely to be able to arrive at a shared and common way of approaching both care and education.

- Parental involvement in the school can have positive spin-off effects for parents themselves. Where parents are invited to become actively involved in the life of the nursery, they gain insights into what it is the workers are doing and why. So, where a school or setting takes time and trouble to explain to parents the reasons for providing play opportunities or why reading to children is important, for example, parents themselves learn and may be able to implement some of what they have learned at home.
- Parental involvement in the school can have positive spin-off effects for teachers and workers. Where parents are actively involved in the nursery, workers have the opportunity to learn more about the parent and child, about the values and principles operating within the child's life out of the setting. Since one of the underpinning principles of high-quality early learning is building on what children already know and can do, the more that is known about the child's life in all its aspects, the better the provision within the nursery or setting is likely to be.
- Parents can offer workers and teachers support. Where partnerships with parents are established, the support of parents can be a powerful tool when change and improvement are sought. There are many examples of parents taking action in order to ensure that a playgroup acquires better premises or in supporting workers' requests for better pay and conditions.

Implications of this for settings

It is clear from this that establishing a close and respectful attitude between parents and workers is crucial to the well-being of the children. Research shows that all parents, regardless of class or cultural group or social position, want what is best for their children. Let us repeat that all parents are keen to help their children and many will give up a great deal to see their children succeed.

One of the difficulties, however, is that there are parents who do not know the best way in which to do this and who lack the confidence to approach staff. There are also many parents who have a limited command of English and who are often dependent on getting a second-hand version through translation. These may be very real barriers to establishing partnerships and are issues that are certainly worth addressing. This places some responsibility on settings to help parents know that the staff in the setting are approachable, keen to listen and eager to help.

This brings us to another very real barrier: the attitude of staff to parents. Where parents are perceived as being 'too pushy' or 'not interested', establishing relationships can be difficult. It is worthwhile examining your own attitudes to the parents of the children in your setting and seeing if you can honestly define parents who make you uncomfortable for one reason or another.

Think about this example of what Martha, a playgroup practitioner, said about her responses to one parent and then try to work out what it is that makes you uncomfortable about a parent or a group of parents and think of ways in which you can overcome your prejudice.

I realised that Tommy's mother made me feel very uncomfortable. She is a teacher and very confident. Every day she would come in and ask what Tommy had done that day. I always felt that she was critical, although she never actually said anything critical. I used to dread open evenings. Then the organiser of the playgroup suggested that we had some social occasions for parents where we invited a small group of parents in to talk about their expectations for their children. We tried to plan groups that were very mixed, and in the group with Tommy's mother was a mother who speaks Turkish, a single parent and a very young mother. I started by telling them what we were planning and what our aims were and then asked for their comments. I was really surprised when Tommy's mother said that she was hoping that Tommy would develop his self-confidence and his independence and his ability to get on with children of his own age. She said she was very happy with his progress at the playgroup and she reassured the very young mother, whose child had only just joined. And she was really nice to the Turkish mother and showed her pictures of what the children had been doing. I had to revise my opinion of her!

How to involve parents as equal partners

We may not all manage to do as much as the settings in Reggio Emilia, but there are many things we already do and many things we might consider doing to help build genuine partnerships.

Home visiting

It is recognised that moving away from home for the first time is traumatic for both child and parent. Many schools and nurseries try to reduce the level of stress by visiting the child and parent at home before the child actually starts in the setting. The obvious advantage of this is that the initial contact takes place in a situation which is familiar and where the parent is in control. But this is a sensitive area and there may well be parents who do not want to be visited at home – particularly where the parent is living in temporary accommodation or where the parent sees the visit as a way for outsiders to assess the 'quality' of the home and of the parents. The rights of parents to refuse a visit should be respected, and it is important that the school or setting be clear about the purpose of the visit and able to explain this to parents.

Think about what you can learn from what one nursery teacher said about how she sees the purpose of home visits:

It is our policy that each child gets this opportunity to meet me in the safety of her/his home environment. . . . I usually take a puzzle, a book, some drawing material and a photo book with pictures of the team, the school, our class, and the children at work. We look through this book together, often with grandparents, aunts and uncles, as well as parents and the child and siblings. I chat a bit about the kinds of things children can do in our class. The pictures speak for themselves when I am unable to communicate in the family's language. That, and a great deal of body language, smiles, gestures usually gets the message across.

During the visit I also take some photographs of the child. They are used later when the child comes to school to make her/his space on the coat hooks, the towel hook and the third, a whole-body one, for the magnet board. The home visit is a good opportunity to ask the parents to write their child's name in the family's language. . . . From there I can enlarge it on the photocopier at school and use it in our graphics area and anywhere else where the child's name appears in English.

(Voss, in Smidt (ed.) 1998, p. 47)

Visiting the nursery or setting

All children and their parents should visit the setting prior to the child starting. You may want to think about sending an individual invitation to the child and parent, making the visit something special. Many settings find that allowing parents and children to visit as often as possible eases the child's entry to the setting and makes the parent feel more comfortable. It is important to try to ensure that not too many new children and parents visit at one time. The best way of making parents and children feel important and valued is to allow one member of staff (perhaps the key worker) time to be able to talk to both parent and child. It is worth considering the point that these initial visits are going to be the time when the parent or carer forms her or his initial impression of the setting, so it is important that they are carefully planned for.

Settling in

Some children find the transition from visiting to attending the setting on a permanent basis easy; others – as you will well know – find it difficult. The child's distress will convey itself to the parent and this may damage the relationship with the setting. You will want to consider your settling-in arrangements with care. Most settings invite (indeed often insist) that parents stay with children at least for the first few days. You will want to think about how you handle this with parents who cannot manage because of work or domestic commitments. The presence of parent or carer is reassuring for the child, and if you want parents or carers to be able to stay with the child, you need to give them adequate notice of this. Most settings also advise parents to tell children when they are leaving and not just to disappear.

Staying in touch

Parents leaving young children in the care of others feel that they are missing out on significant moments in their child's development. You will have read in an earlier chapter how the nurseries in Reggio Emilia keep parents in touch with what their children have done each day. There are many different ways of doing this – from wall displays to link books that go between home and setting to informal chats at the start or the end of the day. In addition to this you will want to ensure that you arrange particular times when parents can come in and have an in-depth discussion about their child's progress. Do remember that the timing of this is important. If you have evening meetings there may be parents who will not attend. Similarly, meetings during the day will exclude some parents. You need to work with parents to find out what is the best time for them and to do your best to meet this.

Involving parents in assessing progress

Parents need and should be involved in both commenting on what they observe about their child's progress and development at home and contributing to what workers observe about development within the setting. You will need to ensure that you involve parents in the Foundation Stage Profile, as described in Chapter 9.

Involving parents in the day-to-day life of the setting

Many nurseries and playgroups invite parents in to help during the day. This help may vary from reading to children to cooking with them or accompanying them on outings and so on. However parents are involved, it is important that their role be clearly spelled out to them so that they know what it is they are doing and why. This implies that workers will have to talk to parents about what they are doing and why. This is one of the best ways of genuinely involving parents in the life of the nursery. You may invite a parent in for a specific purpose – perhaps a mother who has just had a new baby or a father who is a nurse. Again, an explanation of what you want them to do on this visit is important.

Home–school projects

Many settings try to find ways of offering parents things to do at home to build on what has happened in the nursery or setting during the week. Parents may be invited to take home books to read with children or to borrow toys from a toy library. An initial meeting with new parents to introduce the materials and explain ways in which they may be used is useful for parents who may feel reluctant to do things that they see as 'not their role'.

Offering learning opportunities to parents

Some nurseries place great emphasis on their role in educating parents. Some are able to offer parents classes ranging from what to do about temper tantrums or bed-wetting to classes in English as an additional language. This is, of course, very dependent on your resources, but if you have a spare room in your setting you might want to consider offering such classes. It is essential, however, to remember that educating parents needs to be done on the basis of a partnership and not in any patronising or paternalistic way. Programmes offered should ideally be in response to the things that parents express a need to know more about.

Summary
- A great deal has been written about the importance of partnerships with parents. Partnership with parents is fundamental to a successful learning environment for all children, but particularly for children in their first steps away from home.
- All parents want the very best for their children.
- All parents are crucial in the education and development of their own children.
- A partnership with parents, based on mutual respect, will benefit everyone concerned.
- Parents need to be made to feel that they are worth listening and talking to.
- Settings need to ensure that the environment is welcoming to all parents and that all parents know that successful education is a joint enterprise.
- The ways in which parents can become involved need to be clear and explicit.
- Parents' fears need to be acknowledged.

continued on next page

- Workers need to ensure that they are willing to give information, but equally willing to receive it.
- Settling-in procedures need to be carefully considered and explained to parents.
- Settings need to decide how they will ensure that parents with little or no English are not disadvantaged.
- Sometimes, having a theme based on the observed interests of the children allows settings to establish strong partnerships with parents, particularly where the theme selected provides opportunities for parents to contribute their own skills, their knowledge, their talents and their experience.

Bibliography

Children's books referred to

Ahlberg, J. and Ahlberg, A. (1981) *Peepo*, London, Puffin.

Burningham, J. (2001) *Mr Gumpy's Outing*, London, Red Fox.

Cooke, T. (1994) *So Much*, London, Walker Books.

Hawkins, C. (2003) *What's the Time, Mr Wolf?*, London, Egmont Books.

Hutchins, P. (1997) *Titch*, London, Red Fox.

Mansell, D. (1993) *My Old Teddy*, London, Walker Books.

McKee, D. (1982) *Not Now, Bernard*, London, Sparrow Books.

Rosen, M. (2004) *Michael Rosen's Sad Book*, London, Walker Books.

Sharratt, N. and Tucker, S. (2005) *The Three Billy Goats Gruff*, London, Macmillan.

Abbott, L. and Langston, A. (eds) (2004) *Birth to Three Matters: Supporting the Framework of Effective Practice*, Maidenhead, Open University Press.

Abbott, L. and Nutbrown, C. (eds) (2001) *Experiencing Reggio Emilia: Implications for Pre-school Provision*, Buckingham, Open University Press.

Abbott, L. and Rodger, R. (eds) (1994) *Quality Education in the Early Years*, Buckingham, Open University Press.

Ackers, J. (1994) '"Why Involve Me?" Encouraging Children and Their Parents to Participate in the Assessment Process', in L. Abbott and R. Rodger (eds), *Quality Education in the Early Years*, Buckingham, Open University Press.

Allery, G. (1998) 'Observing Symbolic Play', in S. Smidt (ed.), *The Early Years: A Reader*, London, Routledge.

Anning, A. and Edwards, A. (eds) (1999) *Promoting Children's Learning from Birth to Five: Developing the New Early Years Professional*, Buckingham, Open University Press.

Athey, C. (1990) *Extending Thought in Young Children*, London, Paul Chapman Publishing.

Bartholomew, L. and Bruce, T. (1994) *Getting to Know You: A Guide to Record Keeping in Early Childhood Education and Care*, London, Hodder and Stoughton.

Bernstein, B. (1974) *Class, Codes and Control*, London, Routledge and Kegan Paul.

Bragg, S. (1998) 'Talk and Technology', in S. Smidt (ed.), *The Early Years: A Reader*, London, Routledge.

Brooker, L. (2002) *Starting School: Young Children Learning Cultures*, Buckingham, Open University Press.

Browne, A. (1996) *Developing Language and Literacy 3–8*, London, Paul Chapman Publishing.

Bruce, T. (1987) *Early Childhood Education*, Sevenoaks, Hodder and Stoughton.

Bruce, T. (1991) *Time to Play in Early Childhood Education*, Sevenoaks, Hodder and Stoughton.

Bruner, J. (1980) *Under Five in Britain*, London, Grant McIntyre.

Dahlberg, G., Moss, P. and Spence, A. (2004) *Beyond Quality in Early Education: Postmodern Perspectives*, London, RoutledgeFalmer.

David, T. (1990) *Under Five – Under Educated*, Buckingham, Open University Press.

Davies, B. (1989) *Frogs and Snails and Feminist Tales*, London, Allen and Unwin.

Department for Education and Employment (1996a) *The Next Steps*, London, DfEE.

Department for Education and Employment (1996b) *Code of Practice on the Identification and Assessment of Special Educational Needs*, London, DfEE.

Department for Education and Employment (1998) *The National Literacy Strategy*, London, HMSO.

Department for Education and Employment and Qualifications and Curriculum Authority (2000) *Curriculum Guidance for the Foundation Stage*, London, DfEE and QCA.

Department for Education and Skills (2002) *Revised Code of Practice on the Identification and Assessment of Special Educational Needs*, London, DfES.

Department for Education and Skills (2003) *Foundation Stage Profile: Handbook*, London, DfES.

Department for Education and Skills (2004a) *Every Child Matters*, London, DfES.

Department for Education and Skills (2004b) *Birth to Three Matters*, London, DfES.

Department of Education and Science (1977) *A New Partnership for Our Schools* (the Taylor Report), London, DES.

Department of Education and Science (1978) *Special Educational Needs* (the Warnock Report), London, HMSO.

Department of Education and Science (1990) *Starting with Quality* (the Rumbold Report), London, DES.

Devereux, J. (1996) 'What We See Depends on What We Look For: Observation as Part of Teaching and Learning in the Early Years', in S. Robson and S. Smedley (eds), *Education in Early Childhood*, London, David Fulton.

Dombey, H. (1999) 'Questioning Phonics', *Literacy Today*, no. 20: 14–15.

Dombey, H. and Meek, M. (eds) (1994) *First Steps Together: Home–School Early Literacy in European Contexts*, Stoke-on-Trent, Trentham Books.

Donaldson, M. (1978) *Children's Minds*, London, Fontana.

Drummond, M.J. (1994) *Assessing Children's Learning*, London, David Fulton.

Drummond, M.J. (1998) 'Observing Children', in S. Smidt (ed.), *The Early Years: A Reader*, London, Routledge.

Dunn, J. (1988) *The Beginnings of Social Understanding*, Oxford, Basil Blackwell.

Dyson, A.H. (1993) *The Social Worlds of Children Learning to Write in an Urban Primary School*, New York, Teachers College Press.

Dyson, A.H. (1997) *Writing Superheroes: Contemporary Childhood, Popular Culture, and Classroom Literacy*, New York, Teachers College Press.

Early Years Curriculum Group (1992) *First Things First*, Lichfield, Boon Printers.

Elkind, D. (1986) 'Formal Education and Early Childhood Education: An Essential Difference', *Phi Delta Kappa*, 67(9): 631–636.

Faust, H. (2004) *Animated Stories for Young Mathematicians*, London, BEAM Education.

Gardner, H. (1993) *Frames of Mind: The Theory of Multiple Intelligences*, New York, Basic Books.

Goldschmied, E. and Jackson, S. (1994) *People under Three*, London, Routledge.

Goswami, U. (1993) 'Towards an Interactive Analogy Model of Reading Development: Decoding vowel graphemes in beginning reading', *Journal of Experimental Child Psychology*, 56: 443–475.

Gréco, P. (1962) 'Quantité et quotité', cited in C.K. Williams and C. Kamii (1986) 'How Do Children Learn by Handling Objects?', *Young Children*, 42(1): 23–26.

Gregory, E. (1996) *Making Sense of a New World: Learning to Read in a Second Language*, London, Paul Chapman Publishing.

Gregory, E. and Biarnes, J. (1994) 'Tony and Jean-François: Looking for Sense in the Strangeness of School', in M. Meek and H. Dombey (eds), *First Steps Together: Home–School Early Literacy in European Contexts*, Stoke-on-Trent, Trentham Books.

Gregory, E., Long, S. and Volk, D. (eds) (2004) *Many Pathways to Literacy: Young Children Learning with Siblings, Grandparents, Peers and Communities*, London, RoutledgeFalmer.

Gura, P. (ed.) (1992) *Exploring Learning: Young Children and Block Play*, London, Paul Chapman Publishing.

Gura, P. (1996) 'An Entitlement Curriculum for Early Childhood', in S. Robson and S. Smedley (eds), *Education in Early Childhood*, London, David Fulton.

Hall, N. (1999) 'Young Children, Play and Literacy: Engagement in Realistic Uses of Literacy', in J. Marsh and E. Hallet (eds), *Desirable Literacies*, London, Paul Chapman Publishing.

Hall, N. and Robinson, A. (1995) *Exploring Writing and Play in the Early Years*, London, David Fulton.

Hannon, P., Weinberger, J. and Nutbrown, C. (1991) 'A Study of Work with Parents to Promote Early Literacy Development', *Research Papers in Education*, 6(2): 77–97.

Heath, S.B. (1983) *Ways with Words: Language, Life and Work in Communities and Classrooms*, Cambridge, Cambridge University Press.

Holland, P. (2003) *We Don't Play with Guns Here: War, Weapon and Superhero Play in the Early Years*, Maidenhead, Open University Press.

Isaacs, S. (1930) *Intellectual Growth in Children*, London, Routledge and Kegan Paul.

Karmiloff-Smith, A. (1994) *Baby, It's You*, London, Random House.

Katz, L. (1988) 'What Should Young Children Be Doing?' *American Educator*, Summer, 28–45.

Katz, L.G. (1998) 'Introduction: What Is Basic for Young Children', in S. Smidt (ed.), *The Early Years: A Reader*, London, Routledge.

Kearney, C. (2003) *The Monkey's Mask: Identity, Memory, Narrative and Voice*, Stoke-on-Trent, Trentham Books.

Kenner, C. (2004a) 'Community School Pupils Reinterpret Their Knowledge of Chinese and Arabic for Primary School Peers', in E. Gregory, S. Long and D. Volk (eds), *Many Pathways to Literacy: Young Children Learning with Siblings, Grandparents, Peers and Communities*, London, RoutledgeFalmer.

Kenner, C, (2004b) *Becoming Biliterate: Young Children Learning Different Writing Systems*, Stoke-on-Trent, Trentham Books.

Kidner, J. (1988) 'Under Fives', in A. Cohen and I. Cohen (eds), *Early Education: The Pre-school Years*, London, Paul Chapman Publishing.

Kress, G. (1997) *Before Writing: Rethinking the Paths to Literacy*, London, Routledge.

Lanigan, G. (1998) 'Children Playing with Magnets', in S. Smidt (ed.), *The Early Years: A Reader*, London, Routledge.

Leask, J. (2001) 'Sam's Invisible Extra Gear: A Parent's View', in L. Abbott and C. Nutbrown (eds), *Experiencing Reggio Emilia: Implications for Pre-school Provision*, Oxford, Oxford University Press.

Long, P. (1996) 'Special Educational Needs', in S. Robson and S. Smedley (eds), *Education in Early Childhood*, London, David Fulton.

McClellan, D. and Katz, L. (1992) 'Assessing the Social Development of Young Children: A Checklist of Social Attributes', *Dimensions of Early Childhood*, 21(2): 9–10.

MacGilchrist, B. (1992) *Managing Access and Entitlement in Primary Education*, Stoke-on-Trent, Trentham Books.

MacNaughton, G. (2000) *Rethinking Gender in Early Childhood Education*, London, Paul Chapman Publishing.

Malaguzzi, L. with Gandini, L. (1995) 'History, Ideas and Basic Philosophy', in C. Edwards, L. Gandini and G. Forman (eds), *The One Hundred Languages of Children*, Norwood, NJ: Ablex Publishing Corporation.

Marsh, J. and Hallet, E. (eds) (1999) *Desirable Literacies*, London, Paul Chapman Publishing.

Matthews, J. (1994) *Helping Children to Draw and Paint in Early Childhood*, London, Hodder and Stoughton.

Maxwell, S. (1996) 'Meaningful Interaction', in S. Robson and S. Smedley (eds), *Education in Early Childhood*, London, David Fulton.

Melhuish, E.C. (2004) *Child Benefits: The Importance of Investing in Quality Childcare*, London, Daycare Trust.

Moyles, J. (1988) *Just Playing? The Role and Status of Play in Early Childhood Education*, Milton Keynes, Open University Press.

Moyles, J. (1998) 'To Play or Not to Play? That Is the Question!', in S. Smidt (ed.), *The Early Years: A Reader*, London, Routledge.

Nash, M. (1997) *Fertile Minds*, London, Paul Chapman Publishing.

Pahl, K. (1999) *Transformation: Meaning Making in Nursery Education*, Stoke-on-Trent, Trentham Books.

Paley, V.G. (1984) *Boys and Girls: Superheroes in the Doll Corner*, Chicago, University of Chicago Press.

Paley, V.G. (1986) 'On Listening to What Children Say', *Harvard Educational Review*, 56(2): 122–131.

Paley, V.G. (1995) *Kwanzaa and Me: A Teacher's Story*, Cambridge, MA, Harvard University Press.

Rinaldi, C. (2006) *In Dialogue with Reggio Emilia: Listening, Researching and Learning*, London, Routledge.

Robson, S. (1996) 'Home and School: A Potentially Powerful Partnership', in S. Robson and S. Smedley (eds), *Education in Early Childhood*, London, David Fulton.

Rogoff, B. (1990) *Apprenticeship in Thinking: Cognitive Development in Social Context*, Oxford, Oxford University Press.

School Curriculum and Assessment Authority (1996), *Desirable Outcomes for Children's Learning on Entering Compulsory Education*, London, Department for Education and Employment.

Siraj-Blatchford, I. (1994) *The Early Years: Laying the Foundations for Racial Equality*, Stoke-on-Trent, Trentham Books.

Smedley, S. (1996) 'Working for Equality and Equity', in S. Robson and S. Smedley (eds), *Education in Early Childhood*, London, David Fulton.

Smidt, S. (ed.) (1998a) *The Early Years: A Reader*, London, Routledge.

Smidt, S. (1998b) *Guide to Early Years Practice*, 2nd edition, London, Routledge.

Smidt, S (2006) *The Developing Child in the 21st Century: Global Perspectives on Child Development*, London, Routledge.

Smith, M. (1998) 'Making Honey', in S. Smidt (ed.), *The Early Years: A Reader*, London, Routledge.

Sutherland, P. (1992) *Cognitive Development Today: Piaget and His Critics*, London, Paul Chapman Publishing.

Tizard, B. and Hughes, M. (1984) *Young Children Learning*, London, Fontana.

Tizard, B., Blatchford, B., Burke, J., Farquar, C. and Lewis, I. (1988) *Young Children at School in the Inner City*, London, Lawrence Erlbaum.

Tobin, J.J., Wu, D.Y.H. and Davidson, D.H. (1989) *Preschool in Three Cultures*, New Haven, CT: Yale University Press.

Trevarthen, C. (1998) 'The Child's Need to Learn a Culture', in M. Woodhead, D. Faulkner and K. Littleton (eds), *Cultural Worlds of Early Childhood*, London, Routledge with the Open University.

Voss, B. (1998) 'Supporting Young Children', in S. Smidt (ed.), *The Early Years: A Reader*, London, Routledge.

Vygotsky, L. (1978) *Mind in Society: The Development of Higher Psychological Processes*, Cambridge, MA, MIT Press.

Walkerdine, V. and girls from the Mathematics Unit (1989) *Counting Girls Out*, London, Virago.

Weiner, G. (1985) *Just a Bunch of Girls*, Buckingham, Open University Press.

Weis, D. and Worobey, J. (1991) 'Sex-Roles and Family Scripts in Early Childhood', *Early Child Development and Care*, 77: 109–114.

Wells, G. (1987) *The Meaning Makers: Children Learning Language and Using Language to Learn*, Sevenoaks, Hodder and Stoughton.

Whitehead, M. (1997) *Language and Literacy in the Early Years*, 2nd edition, London, Paul Chapman Publishing.

Willan, J., Parker-Rees, R. and Savage, J. (eds) (2004) *Early Childhood Studies*, Exeter, Learning Matters

Woodhead, M., Faulkner, D. and Littleton, K. (eds) (1998) *Cultural Worlds of Early Childhood*, London, Routledge with the Open University.

Websites

The Effective Provision of Pre-School Education (EPPE):
  http://k1.ioe.ac.uk/schools/ecpe/eppe/
Every Child Matters: change for children:
  http://everychildmatters.gov.uk/

Birth to Three Matters:
   http://www.surestart.gov.uk/resources/childcareworkersd/birthtothreematters/
Foundation Stage:
   http://www.surestart.gov.uk/improvingquality/ensuringquality/foundationstage/
Sure Start:
   http://www.surestart.gov.uk

Early Years Foundation Stage: Direction of Travel:
   http://www.everychildmatters.gov.uk/_files/4C9A11CE243627228F27EA46CAC
   3F658.pdf

Index